The Political Theory of

HANNAH ARENDT

In Search of Humane Politics

Toshio Terajima

FUKOSHA

Published by Fukosha Publishers Ltd.
1-3-2 Kanda-sarugakucho, Chiyoda-ku, Tokyo
101-0064 JAPAN

Printed in Japan
ISBN978-4-86258-140-2
First Edition 2021

Contents

Preface

The six articles in this book are papers I have written over more than 20 years. Although I started my study of political theory in the early 1970s and have written almost all my works in Japanese, in the case of Hannah Arendt, I wrote several articles in English. Like Arendt, English is not my mother tongue. An upside to writing in a language other than one's mother tongue is that one can express what one has to say directly in the target language. Although it is a challenge for me to write in English, I feel it is my responsibility to effectively offer viewpoints on Arendt as a Japanese researcher who has long been engaged in the study of political theory. These articles form part of my studies to develop a framework of her political theory from my own viewpoint.

I explored three themes in this book: (1) the significance of Arendt's political theory for ordinary people in our time, (2) biographical elements that formed her thoughts on politics, and (3) the conceptual development of her theory, particularly concerning theories of nonviolence, civil disobedience, and democracy.

What I attempted to formulate was not only an interpretation of the political theory of Hannah Arendt but also an original framework of its development. In my view, Hannah Arendt's concept of action and the active participation of ordinary people in politics can provide the basis for a theory of humane politics that focuses on influencing macro-level politics through voluntary, nonviolent action at the micro-level, that is, from the grassroots level of actively engaged citizens.

This book clarifies how the purpose of Arendt's political theory was to restore both the perspective of ordinary citizens and the understanding of politics as the participation of ordinary citizens in public affairs. Furthermore, it shows how citizen participation in politics encourages individual initiative, open-mindedness, creative problem-solving, and a sharing of ideas that can benefit all concerned.

Special attention is directed to comparisons between Arendt's thoughts and those of Heinrich Blücher (her husband), Gene Sharp, and Masao Maruyama, as well as Blücher's influence on Arendt and her influence on Sharp and Maruyama. I selected these three intellectuals because I believe they were important in developing Arendt's ideas on the creation of citizen-based politics and clarifying new dimensions of political theory. I hope that my arguments somehow shed light on the little-known aspects of her thought. I will be very happy if this book has some thought-provoking effect on the reader.

The six articles in this book have already been published in journals of the universities where I have worked, except for the second article. For the publication of this book, I have made minor changes and revisions to expressions in the original articles.

Chapter 1, "Citizen Action and Radical Democracy: Toward an Arendtian Transformation of Politics," is a paper presented at the 20th World Congress of the International Political Science Association, held July 9–13, 2006, in Fukuoka, Japan, and published in No. 28 of *Kansai University of Law and Politics* in March 2007.

Chapter 2, "How Hannah Arendt Became a Political Theorist," is based on an unpublished paper written as a draft in the 1980s, when I was engaged in a biographical study of Hannah Arendt. This became the foundation of my dissertation written in Japanese, entitled "Sei to Shiso no Seijigaku: Hanna Arento no Shisokeisei (The Political Theory based on Lived Experiences: Hannah Arendt's Thought Formation)" and submitted to Keio University in 1990. In this article, I demonstrated that there were several moments that determined the development of her political theory.

Chapter 3, "Heinrich Blücher: A Hidden Source of Hannah Arendt's Political Thought," was also part of my biographical study of Arendt. It was written in October 1988 in Japanese, with a revised English version published in Vol. 27 of *Human Sciences* in December 1996. This is the revised and augmented version of that article.

Chapter 4, "The Relevance of Hannah Arendt's Reflections on Civil Disobedience," was originally written in English and published in No. 36 of *Kansai University Review of Law and Politics* in March 2015. I wrote this article to analyze and clarify Arendt's thoughts on conscience and politics from my viewpoint.

Chapter 5, "People Power and Nonviolent Revolution: Hannah Arendt's Influence on Theories of Nonviolence," was published in No. 35 of *Kansai University Review of Law and Politics* in March 2014. In this article, I focus on Arendt's theoretical commitment to theories of nonviolence. As I have also studied nonviolence, I sought to develop her political theory in search of new principles of politics.

Chapter 6, "Hannah Arendt and Masao Maruyama: The Meaning of Politics for Citizens," was published in No. 39 of *Kansai University Review of Law and Politics* in March 2018. In this article, I compare the political theory of Hannah Arendt with that of Masao Maruyama, one of the great Japanese political thinkers, and find common traits that proved to be important to their thinking on political theory.

Regarding these English texts, I should thank several people who helped me improve my original drafts. For the articles on citizen action, the relationship between Arendt and her husband Heinrich Blücher, and civil disobedience, I owe much to Dr. Russell Nieli. For the other three articles, on the way Arendt became a political theorist, her influence on nonviolent theories, and the comparison between Arendt and Maruyama, I am very grateful to Mr. Ron Read, who skillfully improved my drafts. For the last article, I am also grateful to Professor You-Kyung Suh for her helpful comments on an early draft. I must also thank my friend Mr. Katsumasa Nishihara and his collaborator Professor Emeritus William I. Elliott, who read and polished the full text. Without their help, this book could not have been completed.

I

Citizen Action and Radical Democracy:
Toward an Arendtian Transformation of Politics

1. Introduction

Hannah Arendt (1906-75) was one of the 20th century's greatest political thinkers. She was, by her own account, a professional political theorist (1) whose theorizing about politics was a continual dialogue with the great political thinkers of the Western tradition. But her reflections on politics were more than just a reflection on a "great man" tradition of the past — Arendt always believed that political theory had to encompass an appreciation for the experiences of ordinary people and ordinary political actors, and the universal experiences of mankind. No elitist, Arendt held that ordinary people's perspectives on the political world were of crucial importance for understanding the true nature of political action.

Politics was for Arendt above all a human activity that must be understood from the standpoint of the human beings who are part of politics. Her understanding of politics differs from most modern views insofar as she

(1) On October 28, 1964, in the conversation with Günter Gaus, a well-known journalist at the time, Hannah Arendt said, "My profession, if one can even speak of it at all, is political theory." (Hannah Arendt, "'What remains? The Language Remains': A Conversation with Günter Gaus," in Hannah Arendt, *Essays in Understanding 1930–1954*, ed. by Jerome Kohn, New York: Harcourt Brace & Company, 1994, p. 1.)

believed that politics at bottom had to be understood as the micro-level of the participating citizenry rather than from the macro-level perspective of nation-states and the elites who govern them. Much of modern political theorizing is state-centered. In the great political thinkers of the modern era including Machiavelli, Hobbes, Locke, and Rousseau, the focus is on the need for a powerful authority to preserve the peace, and this authority is concentrated at the state level to ensure the safety and security of the people. Politics in this view is all about nations, states and the decisions that are made at the national level and on the international stage of power politics.

But this kind of perspective misses the crucially important dimension of the everyday "life-world" — in German *Lebenswelt* — of ordinary people and citizens. Making the situation even worse is the fact that liberalism had become the dominant ideology in the Western world and according to its tenets the entire economic arena was to be relegated to a private realm excluded from the purview of politics. Politics thus became even more detached from the actual life-world of ordinary people and citizens, for whom the economic arena of labor and production is so important.

The purpose of Arendt's political theory was to restore the perspective of ordinary citizens and the meaning of politics as the participation of ordinary citizens in public affairs. The macro-level of state action, she believed, always needed to be viewed from the micro-level of citizen action. But Arendt could view her work, which in many ways appeared quite radical, as a restoration rather than a new innovation because the perspective on politics that she sought to reestablish was one highly developed by the ancient Greeks for whom political life was the chief aspect of life. She could also draw upon a few modern thinkers like Tocqueville, who saw politics as a process created by self-governing citizens. In most of modern politics, Arendt believed, something had been lost, and this could be restored, she held, by a focus on people's actual lived experiences and by an ongoing dialogue with thinkers of the past who had not lost an understanding for the crucial dimension of citizen participation and citizen action. As Margaret

Canovan has pointed out, it is the characteristic of Arendt's political theory "to articulate experience in this way, to enable people to think consciously what they have been only half aware of, to give them names by which to remember experiences that would otherwise vanish without trace." (2)

From the popular nonviolent uprisings in Eastern Europe to the calls for more participatory democracy and a rebirth of civil society that are echoed in so many areas around the globe, we can see how Arendt's theory of the public sphere finds contemporary resonance. It will be shown in the rest of this article how Arendt's concept of citizen action and the active participation of ordinary people in politics can provide a theoretical basis for a theory of humane politics that focuses on influencing the macro-level of politics through voluntary, nonviolent action at the micro-level, that is, from the grass-roots level of acting citizens.

2. Plurality and Action

The meaning of plurality

A central feature of the human condition for Arendt is human plurality. By this she means simply that not one person but always two or more people live on this earth. The "human condition of plurality," she writes, refers "to the fact that men, not Man, live on the earth and inhabit the world." (3) Plurality also means that humans, in their great diversity, are each unique and non-reproducible. Humans cannot be understood merely as instances of some more general law of behavior without doing violence to the true being of each person as distinct and unique. We are all in some sense one-of-a-kind, non-replicable individuals irreducible to anything else. "Plurality is the condition of human action," Arendt writes, "because we are all the same, that

(2) Margaret Canovan, *The Political Thought of Hannah Arendt*, London: J. M. Dent & Sons Ltd., 1974, p. 7.

(3) Hannah Arendt, *The Human Condition*, Chicago: The University of Chicago Press, 1958, p. 7.

is, human, in such a way that nobody is ever the same as anyone else who ever lived, lives, or will live." [(4)] In part because we are each unique, Arendt didn't believe it possible to define human nature. Our individual uniqueness, she once said, takes on the quality of a non-natural idea that only a god could adequately define. Our uniqueness is such that it is not fully comprehended even by ourselves.

Arendt saw how the moral dimension of the human person could be destroyed in the 20th century by the physical and ideological terror of totalitarian regimes, and she was skeptical of much modern political theory, even theorists such as Locke and Rousseau, whose teachings about ideal states of human beings, lacked, in her judgment, grounding in actual political experience. In search of authentic politics, Arendt was drawn back to the classical political theory of Greece and (republican) Rome rather than to modern political theory, because it was in ancient times, she believed, that the vocabulary of truly authentic politics was first developed out of the rich everyday experience of ancient citizens. In her major theoretical work, *The Human Condition*, she makes it plain that she is concerned with theorizing about a politics of acting and doing that must be distinguished from a more ethereal enterprise like contemplation or reflection on the nature of thought itself. Arendt focuses on the *vita activa* — i.e., the active life of labor, work, and action — not the *vita contemplativa*, "the experience of the eternal" which "has no correspondence with and cannot be transformed into any activity whatsoever." [(5)]

Humaneness as the attitude formed in talk and debate

We become human — and humane — according to Arendt, by participating in the common enterprises and common concerns of other people. Crucial to this enterprise is ongoing conversation and debate. Through talk and debate "we humanize what is going on in the world and

(4) *Ibid.*, p. 8.
(5) *Ibid.*, p. 20.

in ourselves," and it is in this manner that "we learn to be human." (6) We develop our humanity and humaneness in ongoing talk and debate with our fellow human beings. The attitude we develop by this process, however, must be "sober and cool rather than sentimental," (7) if its true effect is to be realized.

Arendt sometimes speaks of the common concerns and common enterprise of people that gets expressed through ongoing conversation and debate simply as "the world" (in contrast to a private, contemplative realm), and it is this world — the world of speech and human conversation — that continues to be subject to controversy and upheaval. "The world lies between people," she writes, "and this in-between — much more than (as is often thought) men or even man — is today the object of the greatest concern and the most obvious upheaval in almost all the countries of the globe." (8) She also uses the word "world" in a slightly different sense as a relationship "between [an] individual and his fellow men." (9) These two concepts of "world" are closely connected with the central idea that the human world is formed out of common concern among people who have gathered together to participate in the ongoing conversation and debate. According to Arendt, life in modern societies is really without a world — without this in-between realm of discussion, deliberation, and debate — because of the disintegrating and alienating features of modern mass society. Modern society lacks the arena for citizens to come together to talk, deliberate, and act in concert, and this loss has been, in her view, inestimable in terms of the harms done to the health of modern political life. A more creative kind of political conversation, Arendt believes, was once developed in the Greek *polis*.

---

(6) Hannah Arendt, *Men in Dark Times*, New York: Harcourt Brace & Jovanovich, 1968, p. 25.

(7) *Ibid.*, p. 25.

(8) *Ibid.*, p. 4.

(9) *Ibid.*, p. 5.

Taking initiative as a beginner

In Arendt's political thought political participation, as an ongoing activity, is more important than the attainment of any concrete goal of political life. It is important, she believed, to maintain citizen action through political participation beyond the achievement of any concrete end. A citizen movement that was too narrowly focused on a single end is to be dissolved once that end is achieved. This problem is avoided if a more universal and open-ended goal is chosen — like environmental protection, world peace, or the protection of human rights — but with such a goal the movement must be pursued beyond each generation. The problem then arises of intergenerational continuity and the need for renewed initiative.

The key to the problem of intergenerational continuity and renewed initiative is solved for Arendt by the simple fact of new human beings coming into the world each with their unique individuality, creativity, and capacity for deliberative action that is theirs by birthright. "Each man is unique," she writes, "so that with each birth something uniquely new comes into the world." (10) Human action she goes on to explain, "has the closest connection with the human condition of natality; the new beginning inherent in birth can make itself felt in the world only because the newcomer possesses the capacity of beginning something anew, that is, of acting." (11)

This "capacity of beginning something anew" is the power of taking initiative. It exists in all human beings potentially, and, as a result, all human beings have the power of achieving something unpredictable. It is possible for all human beings to begin something new, though special courage is often called for in the case of political action — such activity often requires that people care for the state of the world and the welfare of mankind more than for their own life and their personal security. But all human beings are capable of beginning something that is new by the fact of their natality, and on a non-political level, everyone can become a hero or a heroine in their own

(10) *The Human Condition*, p. 178.
(11) *Ibid.*, p. 9.

personal life.

Participating in citizenship activity is a form of "second birth," [12] according to Arendt. Everyone joins fellow citizens as a newcomer in the beginning. "With word and deed we insert ourselves into the human world," Arendt writes, "and this insertion is like a second birth, in which we confirm and take upon ourselves the naked fact of our original physical appearance." "This insertion," she goes on, "is not forced upon us by necessity, like labor, it is not promoted by utility, like work. [But] it may be stimulated by the presence of others whose company we may wish to join." [13] To act in this sense means "to take an initiative," "to begin," "to achieve" (in Greek, *archein, prattein*) — that is, to begin an enterprise and to achieve it. To achieve this purpose, according to Arendt, we must have a sense of personal responsibility, a sense of obligation to our fellow citizens and to the world to achieve a noble purpose and to finish what we have begun. [14]

The collective action and activities of citizens in Arendt's view constitute an "in-between" or mediated world, that is a crucial web of human relationships. "The realm of human affairs," she writes, "consists of the web of human relationships which exists wherever men live together." [15] This mediated web of human relationships is the world of common purpose and common activity, and paradoxical as it may seem, it is the world in which each individual experiences his own uniqueness and individuality. The peer group constituted by the ongoing actions of engaged citizens, according to Arendt, constitutes the "the space of appearance" by which she means the space where everybody can be recognized and admired for their own deeds and speeches in their own individuality. This is the space where one confirms who one is, as an individual and unique being.

---

(12) *Ibid.*, p. 176.
(13) *Ibid.*, pp. 176–177.
(14) *Ibid.*, p. 177.
(15) *Ibid.*, pp. 183–184.

Action and citizen activity

For Arendt it is a fundamental condition of human existence to appear before others in order to establish one's own identity and at the same time confirm the reality of the surrounding world. It is indispensable, she believes, to live in a world of other people to achieve one's humaneness in full. As she writes, "without a space of appearance and without trusting in action and speech as a mode of being together, neither the reality of one's self, of one's own identity, nor the reality of the surrounding world can be established beyond doubt."[16] For Arendt, as for the ancient Greeks — or more specifically the Periclean Athenians — this kind of self-realization in the company of others was most importantly carried forth in the practice of citizen action and participatory democratic politics.

The model of the Greek *polis*, however, would obviously be problematic today in the wake of the much larger scale of governments and polities that exist on the nation-state level. We do not live today in such a small political community as the ancient Greek *polis*. As the size of a political community becomes ever larger it becomes more difficult for ordinary citizens to participate daily and directly in politics. The question that arises here is whether it is possible under modern circumstances to have what might be called a genuine civic life. A grass-roots type of citizen action, however, is still possible in the modern world, and can be seen in many of the reform-oriented movements of the contemporary world, such as the environmental and peace movements.

People who participate in citizen action are usually concerned with some kind of public matter, and such action can change the world. The possibilities of citizenship activity in the modern world are much greater than many people realize, and the effect of such activity can be truly transformative. Citizens acting in public at their free will have an enormous capacity to work and cooperate with others, to build open network-type organizations

(16) *Ibid.*, p. 208.

that include many individuals otherwise unknown. By working together with other citizens previously unknown to us, we are able to creatively solve various problems in the contemporary society that can elude solution by the top-down bureaucratic structures of the modern nation-state.

According to Arendt's theory of political action, in order to realize our true humanity and humaneness it is necessary for us to be concerned with public matters not construed from any self-interest but from the interest of a larger world of cooperating human beings. "In the center of politics," she writes, "is always the care for the world." (17) The radicalism of Arendt's thought is thus seen in its focus on cooperation-directed citizen action that is humanistic and humane. Unlike Kant's humanism, however, Arendt is less concerned about the motive of one's action, since the motive may be mixed. What counts in her eyes is the willingness of people to bear responsibility for the world.

In Arendt's view, the ends pursued by citizen action, while important, are still not as important as the process of public deliberation and action. Arendt specifically rejects an instrumental or teleological view of politics in which only the ends or goals matter. Such a view, she believes, can all too easily lead to the justification of terror and violence to realize one's political ends, as has sadly been the case throughout much of modern politics. Deliberating, debating, and acting in concert with others are all centrally important to the political process, according to Arendt. Process is more important than the ends agreed upon. But it would be a mistake to conclude that Arendt's view is that of a "*politique pour la politique*," as Martin Jay has suggested. (18) Ends count for a whole lot for Arendt, but the means of achieving ends and the process of deliberation whereby ends are decided upon are also important — indeed, more important. Citizens should engage in politics, she believed, not simply as a means for affirming a specific purpose,

(17) Hannah Arendt, *Was ist Politik?: Fragmente aus dem Nachlass*, hrsg. von Ursula Ludz; Vorwort von Kurt Sontheimer, München: Piper, 1993, p. 24.
(18) Martin Jay, "Opposing Views," *Partisan Review*, vol. 65, no. 3 (1978), p. 367.

but to affirm life itself, and to carry out our individual responsibility and obligation to the world.

3. The Citizen as an Equal

Equality as an artificial attribute

Arendt's political theory is rightfully seen as having opened up a new dimension in our understanding of freedom.[19] Her idea of freedom draws heavily upon the experience of the free citizens of the democratic *polis* of ancient Athens, and as such, is far distanced from the idea of freedom found in modern liberalism as exemplified, for instance, by thinkers like John Stuart Mill. As Margaret Canovan explains, "against this almost universally accepted [modern] view that freedom is a feature of private life, Hannah Arendt sets the totally opposed notion that it is located in public life and is a feature of action carried on in the company of one's fellows."[20] Her view of freedom is in many ways anti-modernist and not only conflicts with Mill's understanding of freedom as a private-realm concept, but is equally incompatible with the emphasis of Kant and others on freedom as a problem of the inner world of an individual. For Arendt, freedom is exercised in the political realm by free citizens deliberating and debating over common projects that are seen to further the interests of the world.

Closely tied to her concept of political freedom — a freedom which entails the notion of acting in concert with others — is her idea of political equality. Arendt's concept of equality is also derived largely from the Greek *polis* experience, which she believes has a kind of universal validity for different cultures and times. Unlike Tocqueville, who thought equality was a danger to freedom, Arendt points out that political equality was "originally almost

(19) For example, Margaret Canovan considers Hannah Arendt's understanding of freedom as her most important contribution to political theory (See *The Political Thought of Hannah Arendt*, p. 72).

(20) *Ibid.*, p. 73.

identical with [freedom]" [(21)] — and, in her view, it remains so even today. Equality for Arendt means the equal rights and obligations of equal citizens in an ongoing deliberative process such as that which existed in the ancient Athenian *polis*. But equality in this sense, Arendt is quick to emphasize, is not something natural; human beings are not equal by nature. Some are bigger, some smaller; some very intelligent, others not so intelligent; some are born to riches, others are poor; some have strong leadership qualities, others could simply listen and follow.

Not by nature, but by artificial convention was equality achieved in the Greek *polis*, Arendt explains. Human beings, she writes, "received their equality by virtue of citizenship, not by virtue of birth." [(22)] Humans, in other words, become equal through the law. Freedom and equality are thus "conventional and artificial, the products of human effort and qualities of the man-made world." [(23)] "The equality attending the public realm," Arendt writes, "is necessarily an equality of unequals who stand in need of being 'equalized' in certain respects and for specific purposes." [(24)] Equality is thus not an attribute of nature but an attribute of the in-between world of social interaction and political deliberation. But according to Arendt, equality is the precondition of real freedom, for if one is not equal in the political realm one cannot be free.

Equality in the public realm

The idea that equality is a feature of the public realm is exemplified in Arendt's view by the contrast between the Greek household and the Greek *polis*. In the Greek household — the private realm — inequality prevailed with the male head of household ruling over his wife, children, and slaves as a dictator or even tyrant. The private household realm was governed

---

(21) Hannah Arendt, *On Revolution*, New York: The Viking Press, 1963, p. 23.
(22) *Ibid.*, p. 23.
(23) *Ibid.*, p. 23.
(24) *The Human Condition*, p. 215.

by a principle of command and obedience. But in the public realm Greek male citizens engaged with others as equals seeking neither command nor obedience. Regardless of their social position, family background, age, or other personal features, citizens were all equal. The Athenian citizen was neither king nor subject. As Arendt explains, "To be free meant both not to be subject to the necessity of life or to command *and* not to be in command oneself. It meant neither to rule nor to be ruled." (25)

Today, of course, we cannot make the same distinctions that were made in ancient times. There was a double standard in the ancient world that we cannot accept in regard to men and women, free and slave. The concept of political equality that Arendt sees exemplified in the public realm of Greek male citizens is still of value today and merely needs to be expanded so as to include the formerly excluded — the women, the non-citizens, the slaves, etc. Besides the idea of equality itself, what is more valuable in the ancient Athenian understanding of politics as Arendt interprets it is the cardinal importance placed on citizen action, deliberation and debate, and the substitution of persuasion for coercion and violence. What moderns can learn from the ancient Greeks is the importance of deliberative political action, taken by free and equal citizens, who could speak freely and in their own unique voice and seek to persuade rather than command. Freedom, equality, and nonviolent persuasion are features of Athenian citizenship that have enduring relevance for us today.

Five tenets of citizenship and citizen action

The political theory of Hannah Arendt continues to inspire us to address the need to establish norms of citizen action in the modern world. The idea of citizen action and "citizenship education" has attracted the attention of many people in countries like Britain and the United States in recent years where some school curricula have been newly introduced dealing with these

---

(25) *Ibid*., p. 32 (emphasis by Arendt).

subjects. Citizenship, it is sometimes said, has four main attributes: rights, responsibilities, political participation, and political identity.[26] Arendt was particularly concerned with the third attribute of citizenship listed here — participation — and her political theory stresses the need for citizen participation and citizen associations as prerequisites for any kind of authentic public policy making. If we define a citizen as "an individual open to others and society,"[27] we can say that citizen participation and citizenship action is necessary to the health of any decent polity. Even beyond the Greek *polis*, citizen associations, it will be contended here, are needed just as much in the modern world as they were in the time of the ancients. Continuing in this Arendtian mold, I would like to suggest five key attributes of citizen participation and citizen action, each of which is crucial to the formation of vibrant participatory governance.

〔1〕 Spontaneity and creativity are crucial. When citizens are all free and equal and willing to engage in discussion and debate with others, creative and spontaneous responses can emerge from the process of political deliberation. While some participants in the deliberative process will assume a leadership role and take the initiative in proposing new ideas, and to this extent there is an element of inequality in such deliberations, all have the right and the capacity to participate in the decision-making process. And those who take the initiative on one occasion may not be the same as those who assume the initiative on another day when dealing with another topic. Citizen participation fosters creative and spontaneous responses to ongoing political problems.

〔2〕 To take initiative in political deliberation is closely related to the concept of citizen responsibility. Responsibility is closely tied to the belief that one's

---

(26) See Gerard Delanty, *Citizenship in a Global Age*, Buckingham: Open University Press, 2000, pp. 126–132.

(27) Shoji Sano, *Vorantia wo Hajimeru Maeni: Shiminkoekikatsudo* (*Before Beginning Volunteer Activity: Citizen Public-interest Activity*), Tokyo: Koujinnotomo-sha, 1994, p. 37.

words and actions are important, and that one has an obligation to carry through and finish what one has begun. Citizenship responsibility in Arendt's view also requires that citizens care for the well-being of others and the world and make this care the focus of their citizen activity.

〔3〕 Citizenship participation requires participation as equals. Citizens do not place each other under command-obedience type of relationships. Although everyone is not equal in physical strength or intellectual capacity, everyone is unique and all must respect the value and uniqueness of others. Everyone must have a say in the deliberative process, and in order to act cooperatively, it is necessary to have equal relationships among them. For citizenship deliberation to be carried out effectively, it is necessary for it to be anchored in the consciousness of political equality. Everyone must be allowed to participate in the discussion and debate. No one's voice may be privileged over any one else's.

〔4〕 Individuals who participate in politics of deliberation or of discourse must foster a spirit of open-mindedness. Open-mindedness fundamentally means to be open to the criticism of others. Only by being open to such criticism can we hope to eliminate the narrowness and prejudice that is inherent in the human being. Through ongoing deliberation and debate, and through consideration of the critical viewpoints of others, we can help liberate ourselves from the self-interest and one-sidedness that is usually reflected in our own views or in the views embodied in our inherited customs and folkways. None of us is entitled to have a monopoly on truth. No one culture or tradition embodies all there is to know or all that is of value. In the present age of globalization, it is particularly important to foster the ability to understand one another beyond the borders of our own nation and culture.

〔5〕 A sense of justice is also a key component of good citizenship. Here, "sense of justice" simply means the capacity to distinguish right from wrong. We develop our ability to distinguish right from wrong — to determine, that is, what is just and what is unjust — not merely through deliberation with others, but even more importantly, by cultivating our inner capacity of moral discernment and just dealings. To do this it is important to cultivate an independent thinking space in ourselves specifically for this purpose. Cultivating a sense of justice thus requires some degree of reflective or contemplative thinking activity, though it is directed toward the outer world of action and deeds rather than the inner world of religious contemplative self-seeking.

These five tenets of citizen participation and citizen action can be realized even in the modern world in various civic associations dedicated to solving some of the key problems confronted by modern societies. These include such issues as the environment, human rights, the problems of political refugees, homelessness, and poverty. The spontaneity and creativity of voluntary citizens' organizations can provide solutions to such problems that have proven so intractable to the efforts of large, bureaucratic state institutions usually devoid of citizen participation and citizen control. We need to think over what kind of democracy we want to live in, and whether our current form of governance really lives up to the ideal of self-government that most free and cooperative human beings deserve.

4. The Road to Radical Democracy

Arendt's criticism of modern democracy

Since Arendt's model of citizen action and deliberative governance was the Greek *polis*, it is not surprising that she is critical of modern representative democracy. Having witnessed the transition from the Weimar form of representative democracy to the totalitarian regime of Hitler, she knew first-hand that representative democracy could not insure freedom, equality, or the triumph of political wisdom.

Arendt was also critical of the two-party system in Britain and the United States largely because such a system denied direct participation by acting citizens and represented only political interests rather than freely voiced political opinions. At the present time it would be necessary to support calls for greater use of referenda and NPO activity as means of furthering citizen empowerment. The idea of a large-scale representative democracy detached from the participatory presence of thinking, acting, and deliberating citizens was alien to Arendt's political theory, the touchstone of which was discussion and debate among free and equal citizens rather than among political elites.

The word "democracy," Arendt points out, was originally a pejorative term for isonomy (no-rule, in Arendt's translation). "The word 'democracy,'" Arendt writes, "was originally coined by those who were opposed to isonomy and who meant to say: What you say is 'no-rule' is in fact only another kind of rulership; it is the worst form of government, rule by the *demos*." (28) Arendt was very aware, that the demos could become an impassioned mob and be swayed by powerful orators and demagogues — Hitler being a prime example — or otherwise manipulated into conformity by the power of the dominant public opinion. Democracy, she says, can become unstable, because of "the fickleness of its citizens, their lack of public spirit, their inclination to be swayed by public opinion and mass sentiments." (29)

What Arendt really supported was what Margaret Canovan calls "new republicanism" or "radical republicanism," which she understood as a political system in which a citizen becomes "a participator in the *res publica*, sharing in common responsibility for public affairs." (30) This type of republicanism would have some features in common with the republicanism of Rousseau and Machiavelli, but it was distinguished from these by Arendt's belief that participation in public affairs must be voluntary. Arendt was also critical of modern resort to violence to found new republics and was skeptical of certain types of patriotic appeals, as one might expect from someone who had seen the great crimes committed in the name of patriotism in both the

(28) *On Revolution*, p. 23.
(29) *Ibid.*, p. 227.
(30) Margaret Canovan, *Hannah Arendt: A Reinterpretation of Her Political Thought*, Cambridge; New York: Cambridge University Press, 1992, p. 224.

First and Second World Wars.

The kind of republicanism Arendt advocated was a far cry from modern mass democracy where citizens lose their capacity to think freely in the face of mass conformity to the dominant public opinion. Her criticism of democracy in this regard was similar to that of Tocqueville. She agrees also with the following text in *The Federalist*: "When men exert their reason coolly and freely on a variety of distinct questions, they inevitably fall into different opinions on some of them." (31) This is not a bad thing for Arendt, but a sign of republican vigor and independence of spirit by unique individuals. The mass conformity engendered by modern mass democracy is incompatible with any genuine concern for the welfare of the society, or any genuine citizen initiative, she believed. Mass democracy stifles reason, initiative, and public spiritedness, according to Arendt, which is why she stressed the need for republican rather than democratic government. The two have been confused, however, since the nineteenth century.

The idea of republican democracy

Although she does not use the term, we can derive from Arendt's thought a theory of what might be called "republican democracy." (32) In the republican tradition from which Arendt draws, the people are empowered, so it is legitimate to speak of democracy ("government by the people"), but the democracy she has in mind is always republican in the sense that citizens always talk, debate, and deliberate among each other with the public good (*res publica*) in mind. It is no accident that Arendt's *On Revolution* was

---

(31) *On Revolution*, p. 227 (quoted from *The Federalist*, no. 50).

(32) See Antonia Grunenberg, "Einleitung," in *Totalitäre Herrschaft und republikanische Demokratie: fünfzig Jahre The Origins of Totalitarianism von Hannah Arendt*, hrsg. von Antonia Grunenberg unter Mitarbeit von Stefan Ahrens und Bettina Koch, Frankfurt am Main: P. Lang, 2003, p. 9. As Iseult Honohan suggests, "the failure of liberal democracy to prevent the rise of totalitarian governments gave a new impetus [to republicanism] in the aftermath of the Second World War" (Iseult Honohan, *Civic Republicanism*, London: Routledge, 2002, p. 119).

popular with many Eastern Europeans who participated in the revolutions of 1989, and it became a source of inspiration to many seeking to move beyond totalitarian governments.

At the heart of Arendt's "republican democracy" is the emphasis on public spiritedness and universal (as opposed to selfish or self-seeking) ideals such as human rights and world peace. Public spiritedness, in her view, leads neither to patriotism nor state-worship but to concern for what is best in the *res publica*. Political participation in the public sphere by civic-minded citizens is at the heart of Arendt's idea of politics with the citizens acting not only to further their collective well-being, but for the sheer "pleasure to be able to speak, to act, to breathe" (Tocqueville). [33] Political activity itself has value for Arendt when engaged in by free and equal citizens and is seen as a vital part of a meaningful and fulfilling human life.

While it is of great value for citizens to engage in politics, at the same time such participation, Arendt believes, must be voluntary. There must be no obligation to participate in politics; its participants must be "self-chosen." She sees the freedom not to participate in politics as one of the valuable contributions of our Christian heritage. The "freedom from politics," she writes, "was unknown to Rome and Athens," and was "politically perhaps the most relevant part of our Christian heritage." [34] This kind of aristocratic voluntarism characterizes Arendt's republicanism, and is seen as necessary to preserve the spontaneity and freedom necessary for genuine deliberation and debate. No one should be coerced into becoming a participating citizen.

In "The Revolutionary Tradition and Its Lost Treasure," the last chapter of *On Revolution*, Arendt extols the council system as "a new form of government that would permit every member of the modern egalitarian society to become a 'participator' in public affairs." [35] While those who joined the council might be spoken of as elites, they were "the only political élite

(33) *On Revolution*, p. 121.
(34) *Ibid.*, p. 284.
(35) *Ibid.*, p. 268.

[that was] of the people and sprang from the people [that] the modern world has ever seen." (36) Those who did not participate were self-excluded, so there could not arise the feeling of alienation and powerlessness that pervades non-republican forms of government. In the council system the people selected were chosen "for their trustworthiness, their personal integrity, their capacity of judgment, [and] often for their physical courage." (37) In this way the council system reconciled equality and authority.

Arendt goes well beyond the ancient Greek ideal of equality in that her theory does not countenance discrimination on the basis of race, sex, social status, or class. The category of who may be a citizen must be expanded to include effectively all adults under the jurisdictions of the laws. In the public political realm — the "space of appearance" — all people confront each other as equals. While people may be very unequal outside the public space of the republican order, within this space all enjoy equal rights for "freedom in a positive sense is possible only among equals." (38)

A final aspect of Arendt's "republican democracy" is the emphasis on cooperation and acting in concert. Liberal democracy can be criticized because of its competitive and adversarial nature where each side seeks to achieve victory and avoid defeat. Republican democracy, on the other hand, emphasizes the element of cooperation. Such cooperation is necessary to achieve genuine social harmony and public virtue. Today, such cooperation is particularly urgent in the face of the troubling inroads of competitive market values into the civic and political realm, and the need for transnational cooperation in an age of globalization and increasingly porous borders. In the modern world, it is necessary to cooperate across borders, and such cooperation carries the possibility of a greater recognition of our universal humanity and the opportunity to develop creative solutions to problems such as environmental degradation which afflict all of us around the world.

---

(36) *Ibid.*, p. 282.
(37) *Ibid.*, p. 278.
(38) *Ibid.*, p. 279.

Toward nonviolent democracy

For Arendt the political realm was identified as the realm in which persuasion and other nonviolent activities gain currency in contrast to the many non-political realms where force and violence reign supreme. Both the household, in which slaves and women were ordered about, and the sphere of international relations, where bloody conflicts took place, were seen by Arendt as arenas in the lives of the ancient Greeks that were *not* political. "To be political," she writes, "to live in a *polis*, meant that everything was decided through words and persuasion and not through force and violence. In Greek self-understanding, to force people by violence, to command rather than persuade, were pre-political ways to deal with people, characteristic of life outside the *polis*, of home and family life, where the household head ruled with uncontested, despotic powers." (39) Today we would wish to expand this Greek concept of the political to include much of both the private realm and the realm of foreign relations insofar at least as the principle of nonviolent persuasion can be made to operate in each. Nonviolent discourse and non-coercive persuasion must be made to substitute for brute force.

Arendt recognized that violence is often inevitable when a new state or new regime is formed. This process is perhaps most justified in the case of a revolution whose purpose is the liberation of a people from oppression by a tyrannical power. In such a revolution, she says, violence is often used to bring about "a new beginning, ... to constitute an altogether different form of government, to bring about the new body politic."(40) But Arendt was hesitant to affirm the use of violence in politics even in a revolutionary setting lest it led, as it all too easily can and does lead, to the idea that good ends can justify the use of violent means. She believed in fact that the whole concept of politics as a means-end kind of craftsmanship or fabrication, as an arena, that is, in which rational plans or utopias are carried out in the manner in which a craftsman crafts an artifact, is one fraught with danger and

(39) *The Human Condition*, pp. 26–27.
(40) *On Revolution*, p. 28.

confusion. Such thinking, she believed, easily leads to the pragmatic kind of argument that "you can't make an omelet without breaking eggs," (41) and this type of thinking, she believed, has led in the modern world to the justification of murder on a grand scale. "We are perhaps the first generation," she writes, "which has become fully aware of the murderous consequences inherent in a line of thought that forces one to admit that all means, provided that they are efficient, are permissible and justified to pursue something defined as an end." (42)

Arendt sees Plato's utopian vision of the model city in *The Republic* as a model for all political theory which seeks to eliminate political action and replace it with instrumental rationality. The philosopher-king in *The Republic* makes his *polis* in the way a sculpture makes his statue. Such a process, however, eliminates citizen action, and as the modern age has shown, Arendt argues, this kind of instrumental rationality easily leads to the justification of mass violence and murder. Her criticism of utopian blueprints and instrumental rationality in politics is summed up in the following statement: "Only the modern age's conviction that man can know only what he makes ... brought forth the much older implications of violence inherent in all interpretations of the realm of human affairs as a sphere of making." (43) This has been particularly striking in the series of revolutions, characteristic of the modern age, all of which — with the exception of the American Revolution — show the same combination of the old Roman enthusiasm for the foundation of a new body politic with the glorification of violence as the only means for 'making' it. Marx's dictum that 'violence is the midwife of every old society pregnant with a new one,' that is, of all change in history and politics, only sums up the conviction of the whole modern age and draws the consequences of its innermost belief that history is 'made' by men as nature

(41) *The Human Condition*, p. 229.
(42) *Ibid.*, p. 229.
(43) *Ibid.*, p. 228.

is 'made' by God." [44]

Thus, Arendt believed that the substitution of making for acting, of instrumental rationality for genuine citizen action, made politics degenerate into a means to obtain a supposedly "higher" end. [45] As a thinker who survived the era of totalitarianism, Arendt here was sensitive to the problem of justifying immoral means in politics — she knew that such thinking can all too easily lead to slave labor camps or Auschwitz. When "making" — that is, instrumental rationality — is substituted for genuine political action (citizen action), these kinds of horrors are the typical result.

The separation of power from violence

An important distinction that Arendt makes in her writing is that between violence and power. This distinction is made most sharply in her essay "On Violence." Arendt is particularly critical of the maxim of Mao Tse-Tung whereby it is said that "Power grows out of the barrel of a gun." [46] What can grow out of the barrel of a gun, Arendt contends, is not power but violence, coercion, and force. A man with a gun can indeed force others to comply with his wishes, she argues, but this is not power by definition. Power in her use of the term refers to the potential effects produced by people "acting in concert" to persuade and convince others. [47] Power thus depends upon the number of people who support a policy or a government and their level of conviction and persuasion, not on instruments of violence and coercion like firearms or weapons of war. Violence can be exercised by a single person — in the extreme by a megalomaniacal dictator commanding vast armies of destruction — but power according to Arendt only comes through numbers and conviction — in the extreme case by a whole people all

(44) *Ibid.*, p. 228.
(45) *Ibid.*, p. 229.
(46) Hannah Arendt, "On Violence," in *Crises of the Republic*, New York: Harcourt Brace Jovanovich, 1972, p. 113.
(47) *Ibid.*, p. 143.

united against a single tyrant. She writes: "Power is never the property of an individual; it belongs to a group and remains in existence only so long as the group keeps together." [48] "The extreme form of power is All against One, the extreme form of violence is One against All." [49]

Free citizens working together, according to this view, produce power — people power or citizen power — and this power can transform the world, according to Arendt. This kind of people power grows from people connecting themselves "horizontally" in a network of communication rather than "vertically" in a hierarchy of subordination and command. This view has had a great influence in more recent times on theorists of nonviolent citizen action such as Gene Sharp or Michael Randle. Sharp regards power as "the power of a united people," [50] and asserts that this kind of power has the ability to overthrow even dictators. Randle, whose views have been heavily influenced by Arendt's ideas, stresses the importance of voluntary cooperation as the key to effective collective action. [51] Power, in the Arendtian sense, was clearly on display as a "people power" in the Philippine revolution of 1986, and the East European Revolutions in 1989, and these events have proven that nonviolent revolution, far from being an impractical project envisioned only by dreamers unfamiliar with the real world of power politics, can be both real and effective.

One of the examples that Arendt gives of successful nonviolent citizen action is the Gandhian independence movement in India in the 1930s and 1940s. She admits, however, that nonviolent citizen action is not always effective against the brutal violence of repressive regimes. The nonviolent protest of the Czech people against Russian tanks, she says, was "a textbook case of a confrontation between violence and power in their pure states" [52]

---

(48) *Ibid.*, p. 143.

(49) *Ibid.*, p. 141.

(50) Gene Sharp, *Exploring Nonviolent Alternatives*, Boston: Porter Sargent Publisher, 1970, p. 21.

(51) Michael Randle, *Civil Resistance*, London: Fontana Press, 1994, p. 2.

(52) "On *Violence*," p. 152.

— and it was a case where initially, at least, the tanks won. There is some truth to the claim, Arendt says, that "out of the barrel of a gun grows the most effective command, resulting in the most instant and perfect obedience," [53] as organized violence can sometimes defeat nonviolent citizen action and citizen power. The Gandhian movement, she says, would probably not have been effective if the nonviolent resistance had been against Hitler's Germany rather than the more receptive British parliamentary regime. But the substitution of violence for citizen power achieves victory for a regime at a very high moral, spiritual, and existential cost, Arendt says, and her ideal of republican democracy looks forward to the creation of a political situation where violence is minimized and people power gains maximum strength. Arendt, however, did not believe that armies and police forces could be made to go away any time soon, and while it is possible to create a situation where violence becomes less likely to occur, violence, she believed, would always lurk at the extreme of politics.

5. Conclusion

This paper has tried to recapture Arendt's ideal of republican democracy in order to cherish and develop it. Her ideas concerning republicanism and citizen power are rich in insight and practical implications which are of enormous value to the modern, post-totalitarian world of globalized economies and liberal democracies. While no one would dispute the superiority of the kind of representative democracies that have become dominant in the more economically developed parts of the globe since the collapse of fascism and communism, at the same time, the increasing concentration of power in the hands of professional politicians, the manipulation of mass opinion by powerful news media, the increasing influence of money and self-serving interest groups in modern politics, the growth of mammoth, unresponsive

(53) *Ibid.*, p. 152.

government bureaucracies, and the decline in civic spiritedness among the general population are developments that tear the heart and soul out of democracy and rob it of much of its creative potential. Arendt's focus on citizen action and people power, and her appreciation for the greatness of the participatory republicanism of ancient Athens, is a much-needed corrective to the tendency of modern liberal democrats to celebrate uncritically the superiority of their regimes over totalitarianism. The kind of republican democracy that Arendt envisioned can serve as a powerful corrective to the many ills beset by modern liberal democracies.

In her understanding of politics, not in terms of violence or force but in terms of the public power of citizens who come together on a daily basis to deliberate and exchange ideas, Arendt has found a key antidote to the malaise that afflicts much of modern democracy. The kind of citizen-oriented republicanism that she envisioned is able to spur to the creative potential of many individuals who spontaneously deliberate and work together to focus on the needs of the day. In the republicanism of Periclean Athens, the republican system envisioned by Thomas Jefferson, and the council system Arendt finds models for a radical kind of participatory politics that has continuing relevance for the modern age.

Above all, Arendt's ideas provide the basis for a renewed sense of citizen empowerment and the reconstitution of modern politics from the bottom up. It is only when citizens and citizen action take the initiative and become the driving force in politics that the ideal of authentic democracy — in the sense of "power to the people" — can be effectively realized. The realization of such a politics, where the center of gravity lies in citizen-initiative rather than the power and manipulation of elites, has important advantages. It provides not only greater creativity and humaneness in the formulation of public policy, but also enables ordinary citizens to reap the fruit of political participation, which are not available in the private sphere. Citizen participation in politics encourages individual initiative, open-mindedness, creative problem-solving, and a sharing of ideas that can be of benefit to all concerned.

Although citizen action in Arendt's own thought was limited to territorially-restricted sovereignties — the idea of a sovereign world-state, she once said, "would be the end of all citizenship. It would not be the climax of world politics, but quite literally its end" (54) — we can easily expand upon her idea of citizen participation in the contemporary world to include citizen initiatives beyond nation-state borders. Many of our problems today are transnational in scope — including environmental degradation and climate change, international war, poverty, AIDS, etc. — and they may be most effectively addressed by the cooperative relationships of citizens working both within and between nations. The development of modern transportation and communication provides possibilities for such intra- and transnational citizen initiatives that were certainly not available to Greek citizens in classical times or to the yeoman farmers in Thomas Jefferson's day. Arendt's ideas are rich in implications and possibilities for development, and rather than confronting international politics and the global arena as mere spectators or observers, engaged citizens must take the initiative in addressing problems that cannot be left only to commercial interests, bureaucrats, and professional politicians. We have a responsibility to the world, to speak in Arendtian terms, and this responsibility today must be global in scope.

(54) *Men in Dark Times*, p. 82.

II

How Hannah Arendt Became a Political Theorist

1. Introduction

Awareness of the significance of political theory has greatly increased since the 1970s. Although post-war refugee intellectuals such as Hannah Arendt, Leo Strauss, and Eric Voegelin had published remarkable works, mainstream studies in political science still revolved around scientific inquiry, and it was said that political thought was declining in contemporary times. Students of political thought were actually interested in interpretations of works written by great thinkers of the past, but Arendt was outstanding in demonstrating the ability to analyze political realities without using scientific methods. That is, she showed the way to understanding political issues from the viewpoints of history and thought.

Needless to say, the scientific approach to political issues had developed remarkably in the 20th century, and this enabled us to grasp realities objectively. Although we must admit that the normative study cannot itself replace the scientific study, I believe there is room for political theory within the entire academic discipline of politics. Moreover, we must develop a normative study of politics in order to moderate advances in science and technology, since unchecked development may undermine the sustainability of all species on earth.

In contrast to other academic researchers, Arendt lived a dramatic life — encounters with philosophy, resistance against Nazis, exile to Paris and New York, learning the American political tradition and culture, and observing the Eichmann Trial. These formative experiences can be found behind the basic tenets of her political theory. Her life was partly depicted in the movie titled "Hannah Arendt," (1) which was based on biographical facts but focused only on her experience observing the Eichmann Trial and how she reacted to criticisms of her Eichmann report in the *New Yorker*. The fact that Arendt, as a Jewish philosopher, reacted to the trial as a teller of factual truths — criticizing the collaboration of Jewish councils with Nazis while not condemning the German people — seems to have been used in the film as a rationale for reconciliation between Germans and Jews. I believe, however, the most dramatic period of her life was the eight years from 1933 to 1940, because during these years she struggled against Nazis and experienced the horrors of arrest and internment in a camp in Gurs, France.

Although she wrote about these experiences in neither her memoires nor autobiography, Arendt's political theory was formed by her reflections on the historical events she lived through. What interests me is how she became a political theorist. As is well known, she wrote that she came "from the tradition of German philosophy," (2) although she later said good-bye to philosophy. She broke off her connections to philosophy in 1933, when she left the world of literature and philosophy and entered practical activities. She engaged in such social work as helping young Jews escape from all parts of Europe and emigrate to Palestine. After she settled in America as a refugee intellectual, she engaged in writing on political issues and established her profession as a political theorist.

I would like to consider, therefore, these moments and divide her path to political theory into the following three periods: (1) Encounter with

(1) This is a German-Luxembourgish-French dramatic film produced in 2012, directed by Margarethe von Trotta and starring Barbara Sukowa.

(2) Hannah Arendt, "Eichmann in Jerusalem," (An Exchange of letters between Gershom Sholem and Hannah Arendt), *Encounter*, vol. 22 (January 1964), p. 53.

philosophy: the kind of philosophy that is important for thinking politically; (2) From philosophy to politics: how she was caught up in politics; and (3) From Politics to political theory. If a free-thinking spirit is so important for constructing a political theory, how did she become a political theorist as a vocation? In fact, she formed her character on her own under the circumstances she lived through. I will take up these three historical moments in chronological order.

2. Encounter with Philosophy

As many biographies on Arendt have observed, her life was so dramatic that her way to political *praxis* has attracted many readers. In the 1920s, as Peter Gay wrote in his book, *Weimar Culture: The Outsider as Insider* (1968), "She recalled 'we young students did not read newspapers in those years.'" Arendt admitted this as fact in a response to Gay on his inquiries regarding this description in a manuscript of the book. (3)

Arendt was intimately familiar with the works of Immanuel Kant and immersed in the works of Søren Kierkegaard at the age of 14. (4) The background of her education was the European intellectual milieu. Her closest friend, Anne Mendelssohn, a descendent of Moses Mendelssohn, said that Arendt had "read everything" (5) including contemporary novels not suited for young people and that she was acquainted with the main works of literature in the humanities and philosophy. So crucial was philosophy for the young Arendt that she stated, "I can either study philosophy or I can drown

(3) See Peter Gay, *Weimar Culture: The Outsider as Insider* (1968), p. 70; Hannah Arendt, Letter to Peter Gay, June 15, 1967, in *The Papers of Hannah Arendt*, The Library of Congress, p. 006365.

(4) Hannah Arendt, "What Remains? The Language Remains" (A Conversation with Günter Gaus), in Hannah Arendt, *Essays in Understanding, 1930–1954*, ed. by Jerome Kohn, New York: Harcourt Brace & Company, 1994, p. 9.

(5) Elisabeth Young-Bruehl, *Hannah Arendt: For Love of the World*, Yale University Press, 1982, p. 32.

myself." [6] But what kind of philosophy seized her in her adolescence?

Existential moment

During the period between the two world wars, there was an atmosphere in which one constantly felt near death, since fear of violence penetrated people's consciousness. In Germany, there were riots by the right wing and revolutionary movements by the left wing. The First World War mobilized many people to the battlefield, and in some cases their residential areas also became part of the battlefield. Airplanes were designed and built in 1903 by the Wright brothers in America, and aircrafts were immediately employed for bombing throughout the world.

In contrast to this atmosphere in political society, the 1920s, when Arendt spent her student years, constituted the most stable period of Weimar democracy. As is usual for intellectuals, she felt that engaging in politics would be a burden, and thus she was not concerned with political affairs. It was philosophy that she first loved. She attended the seminar of Martin Heidegger at Marburg University and then that of Karl Jaspers at Heidelberg University. In 1928, she finished writing her dissertation on St. Augustine under Jaspers. After leaving the university, she received a grant and began writing a biography of Rahel Varnhagen, a German Jewess who flourished about a century before Arendt. She continued her studies until she fled from Germany, and in 1938 she finished the Rahel Varnhagen biography in Paris.

In her youth, Arendt was attracted by Kierkegaard, who rejected church teachings and every kind of dogmatism. However, she differed with him on the point of his development of experience philosophy (*Erlebnisphilosophie*); nevertheless, although she did not recount her personal story, her theory is underpinned by her personal experiences. She was moved by his thought that one must live independently of any doctrine or "ism," as shown by his

---

(6) "What Remains? The Language Remains," p. 8.

own works and life. What she learned from the existential philosophy of Kierkegaard was to live independently without relying on any authority.

It is well known that existential thinkers grasp human life as once-ness. The life of a human being is determined by birth and death. Humans can live productively by being self-conscious of death. Each human being, or "*Dasein*" in the terminology of Martin Heidegger, is a being moving toward his/her death. In the case of Kierkegaard, despair and anxiety are determinants in turning around one's life to live positively. But for Arendt, birth and hope are most important. It is in dark times, she finds, that humans have the possibility of beginning something new. We must have hope under such desperate situations as totalitarian domination.

Although humans are mortal, she asserted that the goal of human life is not death but to leave behind a better world when one dies. Arendt stated, "The fact that man is capable of action means that the unexpected can be expected from him, that he is able to perform what is infinitely improbable. And this again is possible only because each man is unique, so that with each birth something uniquely new comes into the world." (7) This statement clarifies her type of existential thought, in which she is concerned with human uniqueness originating in natality. Human beings do not come into the world by their will. "Being in the world" means the condition of being thrown into the world, but one has the potential to make something new and should live by making use of this faculty.

There is a great difference between Arendt's concern with natality and the existentialists' concern with death. Contrary to most of the latter, who are preoccupied with death and want to conquer the despair and loneliness conditioned by death, she emphasizes the human faculty to start something new. By beginning new activity, one can make oneself immortal. Traces that one has lived will remain by one's actions. As Arendt says, though humans

(7) Hannah Arendt, *The Human Condition*, Chicago: The University of Chicago Press, 1958, p. 178.

"must die, they are not born in order to die but in order to begin." [8] What she inherits from existentialism is not thought about death but thought on the uniqueness of human beings, which would later be the foundation of her concept of plurality.

Jewish moment

It is very significant that Arendt was born a Jew and encountered discrimination due to anti-Semitism. Anti-Semitism gradually pervaded society and took the form of exclusionist attacks against Jews throughout the German-speaking countries. Arendt was educated to live with pride by her mother Martha: She was told that if she was humiliated by teachers, she should stand up and leave the class. Then, when she was a student at the girls' gymnasium, at 15 years of age, she was offended by a young teacher for his thoughtlessness. On that occasion "she led her classmates in a boycott of the teacher's classes and was, as a consequence, expelled from school." [9] She was subjected to anti-Semitic discrimination in that period and thus became more and more conscious of her Jewishness.

Arendt chose not to stay at the university after earning her doctorate from Heidelberg University in 1928, with her dissertation on "The Concept of Love in Augustine." Since she was a Jew, it was nearly impossible to get a position at a university under the conditions of that time. Arendt, however, continued to study. Her primary concern was the Jewish question. She concentrated her attention on the study of Rahel Varnhagen, a Jewish romanticist who had created a Goethe-cult salon in Berlin. Although she felt great empathy with Rahel, it is not appropriate to regard her biography as a proxy autobiography of herself, since Arendt's way of life was quite different from Rahel's way of grappling with the Jewish question, such as renaming or conversion. After she failed in her efforts to identify with her subject, she grasped issues of being Jewish as a social question. However, a

(8) *Ibid.*, p. 246.
(9) *Hannah Arendt: For Love of the World*, p. 34.

political dimension emerged in the last two chapters of the book, which she wrote between 1933 and 1938 while in exile in Paris. She denied assimilation, because she found it impossible for Jews to assimilate into a society that was becoming more and more anti-Semitic. Rahel's situation is thus reflected in Arendt's position of affirming the importance of being a Jew and the need to reject assimilation.

Through the Jewish question, Arendt opened her eyes to politics. However, her concern with history and society was determined before she became engaged in politics. Contrary to contemporary philosophers, she made use of her knowledge to understand the political situation in which Jews were persecuted and expelled. Furthermore, she felt that a crisis was soon coming to the Jewish people and she became increasingly conscious of the international situation.

3. From Philosophy to Politics

It was 1933 when Arendt entered the world of political action. In this sense, 1933 was a decisive year for her. Since she recognized that a large number of German people were behind Hitler as his supporters, she was not shocked by Hitler's assumption of power. But she was shocked by the fact that people around her, intellectuals, got swept up by the wave of *Gleichschaltung* (Nazification of state and society). Although her first love was philosophy, Arendt became disillusioned with philosophy, deciding that education is worthless and vowing never again to "get involved in any kind of intellectual business." (10)

The turning point for Arendt

Before 1933, although she had already opened her eyes to politics,

(10) "What Remains? The Language Remains" (A Conversation with Günter Gaus), in Hannah Arendt, *Essays in Understanding, 1930–1954*, ed. by Jerome Kohn, New York: Harcourt Brace & Company, 1994, p. 11.

Arendt was still apolitical and felt that committing to politics would be a burden and troublesome, as many young students thought at the time. However, when the *Reichstag* was set afire, she felt a responsibility to get involved in politics. Although she was neither Communist nor Zionist, she provided her apartment as a base for protecting Communists who fled from Nazis and accepted with delight the request from German Zionists to collect anti-Semitic materials at the Prussian State Library. She took these actions because she no longer felt she could simply be an observer.

Arendt had to act as a Jew. The shift from observer to actor was motivated by the simple fact that she felt a responsibility to the people of the world. She could not remain the same as before. She correctly understood the essence of the Jewish question through her study of Rahel Varnhagen and reached the insight that she had to fight against the Nazis as a Jew. She identified herself as a Jew, which is the tradition of Jewish writers such as Rahel Varnhagen, Heinrich Heine, Bernard Lazar, and Franz Kafka. They rejected assimilation and affirmed Jewishness, namely, they affirmed belonging to the Jewish people. She reached the recognition that "If one is attacked as a Jew, one must defend oneself as a Jew." [11] Such self-consciousness would be the precondition for her to engage in politics.

In Berlin, this political engagement resulted in her arrest by the Gestapo for anti-Nazi activities. However, she was released after eight days of detention because she encountered a sympathetic policeman. She then fled to Paris illegally without a passport.

The positive meaning of action

In Paris Arendt joined Youth Aliyah, a Zionist organization established to help young Jews emigrate to Palestine. She joined in its staff as a social worker, collaborating with French women in planning and arranging the emigration of the children of Jewish refugees. She worked for the Zionist

(11) *Ibid.*, p. 12.

cause in a practical sense because she believed it was necessary for Jews to have a place to live. In this sense, her connection to Zionism was similar to that of Franz Kafka.

Arendt defined a human being as a man among men (i.e., a person among persons). She writes the Latin words, *inter homines esse* (to be among men) as what it means to live, several times in her works. For the Romans, to live means to be among humans and to die is to cease to be among humans. In the same vein, Arendt extended this concept to the relationships among nations. She often used the expression "nation among nations" in the sense that the Jewish people should be recognized as an equal nation among nations.

In retrospect, Arendt remembered the eight years in Paris as "rather happy years." (12) This means that, contrary to her expectations, she came to know that taking part in public affairs is in itself enjoyable and an important aspect of human life that one cannot experience in one's private life. To act gives one's life fullness. Through acting with others, one can express oneself frankly in one's speech and deeds. Everybody has his or her own uniqueness. Such is the nature of political experience. Since politics is a way of public life, where people cooperate without employing violent means, Arendt herself learned the essence of politics through resistance against the Nazis.

This is the same as the experience of people who participated in the Resistance against Nazi invasion, as retold by the French poet René Char. Arendt recalls such an experience as a treasure, because she wholly gives credit to his statement. According to her interpretation of the words of Char, "*Notre héritage n'est précédé d'aucun testament*" (our inheritance was left to us by no testament), "without premonition and probably against their conscious inclinations, they had to come to constitute willy-nilly a public realm where — without the paraphernalia of officialdom and hidden from

(12) Hannah Arendt, "Sonning Prize acceptance speech" (1975), used as a Prologue to a posthumous collection of her work titled *Responsibility and Judgement*, edited and with an Introduction by Jerome Kohn, New York: Schoken Books, 2003, p. 4.

the eyes and foe — all relevant business in the affairs of the country was transacted in deed and word." [13] Arendt continued, "It did not last long. After a few short years they were liberated from what they originally had thought to be a 'burden' and thrown back into what they now knew to be the weightless irrelevance of their personal affairs, once more separated from 'the world of reality' by an *épaisseur triste*, the 'sad opaqueness' of a private life centered about nothing but itself." [14]

What men of the Resistance aimed to build was a public space in which they could appear as they really are. They could find themselves by engaging in any kind of action. "In this nakedness, stripped of all masks — of those which society assigns to its members as well as those which the individual fabricates for himself in his psychological reactions against society — they had been visited for the first time in their lives by an application of freedom, not, to be sure, because they acted against tyranny and things worse than tyranny...but because they had become 'challengers,' had taken the initiative upon themselves where freedom could appear. 'At every meal that we eat together, freedom is invited to sit down. The chair remains vacant, but the place is set.'" [15]

This realization is something like a treasure. The reason that such action was possible lies in the realization that the resisters were liberated from their private interests and ideological positions. Although it was lost, it was not lost forever. If we keep our memory of the activity, we can revive such an experience and live it again. Arendt felt it necessary to connect such an experience with that of human experiences of the past. For that purpose, she traced events back to the past and tried to recover the real meaning of politics for ordinary people.

---

(13) Hannah Arendt, *Between Past and Future*, New York: The Viking Press, 1961, p. 3.
(14) *Ibid.*, p. 4.
(15) *Ibid.*, p. 4.

4. From Politics to Political Theory

Arendt's experience with the Nazis meant, on the one hand, that she came to know the positive aspect of political engagement. On the other hand, she experienced totalitarianism in Germany. Her friends and relatives were murdered in the Auschwitz concentration camp. She also felt the horror of encountering the secret police and being interned in a camp. What matters to her is not to write her own experiences directly but rather to theorize about them in general terms. Here, theorizing means to grasp the authentic meaning of political phenomena and to find the ideas that are worth being remembered as a way to recover the positive meaning of human experience.

According to her, "the men of European Resistance were neither the first nor the last to lose their treasure." (16) People who unexpectedly participated in revolutions have had similar experiences. Most of them had the feeling of freedom and happiness through taking part in public affairs. What matters is that they not only lost their treasure as soon as they returned to their own private lives but also that they could not give names to these experiences. Therefore, Arendt decided to articulate such experiences by returning to the language of political writers who dictated them in their times. As *theōrein*, which originally means contemplation, from "the Greek notion of the divine," (17) Arendt intended to catch the essence of political matters. This is the task she took upon herself.

According to Dante Germino, although *theōria* (theory) comes from the activity of "seeing" and "the *theōros*, or theorist, was the man whose role it was to be a spectator or onlooker" as at the Olympic games, "with the development of philosophy in Greece, *theōria* took on an additional, a more profound, meaning: it was applied to the act of knowing, or inward seeing,

(16) *Ibid.*, pp. 4–5.
(17) Hannah Arendt, *The Life of the Mind*, vol. 1: *Thinking*, New York: Harcourt Brace Jovanovich, 1978, p. 130.

through the eye of the mind." [18] It is the activity of *periagōgē*, or conversion, which Plato expressed as the conversion of the soul in his famous "allegory of the cave" in *The Republic*. Just as with this traditional mode of thinking, Arendt not only discerned the essence of political phenomena but also tried to redirect our understanding of politics.

Going back to the past

While in *The Origins of Totalitarianism*, published in 1951, Arendt fully depicted the negative aspects of politics, she chiefly describes the positive sides of politics in *The Human Condition* (1958) and *On Revolution* (1963). In *The Human Condition* she revisited the ancient Greek *polis* and rediscovered a prototype of politics. There she posits politics as action, one of three activities. The other two are labor (for sustenance) and work (fabrication of enduring objects). These activities, which she contrasts to contemplation, are aspects of ordinary human life. Accordingly, action is also one aspect of what we do every day.

According to Arendt, action is tightly connected with speech. She goes back to Aristotle's definition of a human being as "*zōon politikon*" and "*zōon logon ekhon*," which are interconnected reciprocally. What Aristotle did was to describe the state of citizens in the ancient Greek *polis*: "To be political, to live in a *polis*, meant that everything was decided through words and persuasion and not through force and violence." [19] This prototype of politics is distinguished by how citizens solve their problems not by violence but by *persuasion*.

The key to her thinking is found in the notion that the most important matter is to set up a public space that allows humans to act. Action is strongly related to the plurality of human beings and the human faculty of beginning something new. Here, everyone is unique, in that there exist no

(18) Dante Germino, *Beyond Ideology: The Revival of Political Theory*, Chicago: University of Chicago Press, 1967, p. 8.
(19) *The Human Condition*, p. 26.

two people who are exactly the same. Moreover, everyone can reveal his or her own uniqueness through action. Arendt states, "Because of its inherent tendency to disclose the agent together with the act, action needs for its full appearance the shining brightness we once called glory, and which is possible only in the public realm." (20)

As suggested by her desire to dedicate *The Human Condition* to Martin Heidegger, there are echoes of the phenomenological approach in that work. The fact that he rejected her offer suggests the difference in the two thinkers' phenomenologies. While Heidegger recognizes humans as thinking beings, Arendt grasps human beings as acting beings. Furthermore, her concept of action is based on her notions of anthropology, that is, her understanding of human beings. To live together, we necessarily need to cooperate with others. Authentic politics is done without violence. Her concept of politics is more positive than the conventional idea. She believes that humans can reveal themselves in action and experience joyfulness and a sense of personal fulfillment. Therefore, it is not the goal of action but the process of action that is important.

In order to show glorious moments of human action, Arendt reviews history and relates her conviction, i.e., that acting is fun, to human experience. Although her knowledge of history is limited to Europe and America, she depicts historical experiences as common ground for a pure type of politics. The Athenian citizens' politics is valuable for all humankind, and its essential aspects reappear in other places and other times.

Public space and public happiness

Arendt turns to brilliant historical moments in *On Revolution* (1963). As expressed earlier, Arendt knew what politics meant through her experiences with totalitarianism. She learned not only the negative sides of politics, such as the secret police and concentration camps, but also the positive sides of

(20) *Ibid.*, p. 180.

politics such as action, public space, and plurality.

"The history of revolutions — from the summer of 1776 in Philadelphia and the summer of 1789 in Paris to the autumn in Budapest in 1956 — which politically spells out the innermost story of the modern age, could be told in parable form as the role of an age-old treasure which, under the most varied circumstances, appears abruptly, unexpectedly, and disappears again, under different mysterious conditions as though it were a fata morgana." (21) She tries to retell the history of councils that spontaneously appeared in the process of revolutions in France, Germany, Russia, and Hungary. She also recalls the imagination of Thomas Jefferson, who envisaged a system of polity based on an elementary republic. The last chapter of *On Revolution* very deftly reminds us of these forgotten facts about people who participated in politics through their sheer will.

Jefferson's imagined ward system was a new type of governmental system based on an elementary republic limited by space and population, for there is an adequate size of polity in which everybody can participate. What he expected of wards was "to permit the citizens to continue to do what they had been able to do during the years of revolution, namely, to act on their own and thus to participate in public business as it was being transacted from day to day." (22)

The point of remembering the council system is that it is a public space in which everyone can participate. It is a hope "for a transformation of the state, for a new form of government that would permit every member of the modern egalitarian society to become a 'participator' in public affairs." (23)

The council system is different from the representative system in that people can participate at the lowest level of a council and discuss common

(21) *Between Past and Future*, p. 5.

(22) Hannah Arendt, *On Revolution*, New York: The Viking Press, 1963, p. 254. Arendt borrows the term "elementary republic" from a letter by Thomas Jefferson to Joseph C. Cabell (February 2, 1816) in order to express the lowest level of the counsel system, public space in which ordinary people can spontaneously take part.

(23) *Ibid.*, p. 268.

matters of the nation in a direct way. They speak and act as equals. They voluntarily take part in the council but enjoy the right not to participate in it. While in the representative system representatives are often elected by "sales talk," in the council system council participants arise from the people and are chosen to join the upper council by the principle of confidence. The elementary republic, namely the council in the region or workplace, provides people with a public space where they can appear before others.

According to Arendt's explanation, "From these 'elementary republics,' the councilmen then chose their deputies for the next higher council, and these deputies, again, were selected by their peers, they were not subject to any pressure either from above or from below. Their title rested on nothing but the confidence of their equals, and this equality was not natural but political, it was nothing they had been born with; it was the equality of those who had committed themselves to, and now were engaged in, a joint enterprise. Once elected and sent into the next higher council, the deputies found themselves again among the peers, for the deputies on any given level in this system were those who had received a special trust." (24) These people could engage in the activities of "expressing, discussing and deciding" (25) by reflecting the common thinking of society.

Although she presented the council system as an alternative to the representative system, as she stated, "The common object was the foundation of a new body politic, a new type of republican government which would rest on 'elementary republics' in such a way that its own central power did not deprive the constituent bodies of their original power to constitute." (26) What Arendt really wanted was to recollect the memory of "the space of

(24) *Ibid.*, p. 282.

(25) *On Revolution*, p. 238. See also Jefferson's letter to Samuel Kercheval, July 12, 1816 in Thomas Jefferson, *The Complete Works of Thomas Jefferson: Autobiography, Correspondence, Reports, Messages, Speeches and Other Official and Private Writings*, ed. by Henry Augustine Washington, Madison & Adams Press (Kindle Edition), 1984.

(26) *Ibid.*, p. 271.

men's free deeds and living words"[27] and thus to let public space reappear in the contemporary world. Since action is the fundamental condition for humans, it is crucial to create such a public space as to foster human action in cooperation with others wherever we live.

One can find positive values in the process of action. Arendt discovered the expression "public happiness" in the writings of the Founding Fathers of the American nation. Through the words of Thomas Jefferson and John Adams, Arendt sought the meaning of public happiness. According to her, "the pursuit of happiness" in the Declaration of Independence meant not only "the pursuit of well-being" but also "being a participator in public affairs."[28] These founders were convinced that the men of the American Revolution felt happiness by participating in public affairs.

Where does the feeling of public happiness come from? It comes from the fact that to be seen and heard by other people gives rise to pleasure. John Adams emphasized the need to "have a space where we are seen and can act."[29] Acting itself is a valuable and integral aspect of human life. Arendt learnt this through her activities against the Nazis. Although she was convinced of this notion, she expressed it in such a way as to connect it with the experiences of humans and thus tell the forgotten stories of revolutions vividly.

Periagōgē of political theory

What Arendt did as a political theorist is the *periagōgē* of political theory. Although it originally meant to turn one's mind from focusing on the temporal and the transient to the permanent and universal, in the case of Arendt it meant to shift the meaning of politics from the conventional to the authentic.

Her concepts of politics and power, therefore, have duality: In *The*

(27) *Ibid.*, p. 285.
(28) *Ibid.*, p. 129.
(29) *Ibid.*, p. 133.

Origins of Totalitarianism, she depicted politics as negative phenomena and power as violence. But she did not capture the authentic meanings of these words in the realities of totalitarian domination, which negates human plurality, public freedom, and public space. Already in this work one can find her positive concept of politics. She defined power as the capability to act in concert and to engage in a common enterprise. She understood freedom as the ability to act in public as well as to begin something new. She ends the *magnum opus* by quoting Augustine's words "*Initium ut esset homo creatus est*" (That a beginning be made, man was created) and indicating that "this beginning is guaranteed by each new birth; it is indeed every man." (30)

The reason for duality in Arendt's concept of politics lies in her intention to divert our understanding of politics. But in which direction? Arendt implicitly indicates the direction from state-level politics to citizen-based politics and intends to change politics from the phenomenon of domination to that of no-rule. The politics of no-rule is based on equal relationships among citizens. The core of politics is in freedom. However, freedom cannot fully develop without a guarantee of equality among humans.

According to Arendt, politics is a valuable activity in itself. It must not be the means to a certain end. Humans have every possibility, more or less a potential capability, to attain unpredictable circumstances. We can create a better, more humane world. For that purpose, humans should do their best. Her political theory encourages us to be active for good and to cooperate with others toward a common goal. From Arendt's viewpoint, freedom is the state of action and to be active is to be human. We should take politics back from politicians and return it to ordinary citizens, thus making it an important part of our lives.

---

(30) Hannah Arendt, *The Origins of Totalitarianism*, 3rd edition, New York: Harcourt, Brace & World, Inc., 1966, p. 479.

5. Conclusion

Arendt is concerned with how to recover public freedom and public happiness in the contemporary context. Therefore, she continued to be interested in actual politics. Although after she fled to America she did not engage in political action, she was concerned with the world situation. She never lost the feeling of having a responsibility to the world.

Arendt lived through the totalitarian age and learned both positive and negative aspects of politics. Her political theory is based on 20th-century human experience. It can be said that without her writings, we could not understand the real meaning of the political phenomena of the 20th century, and her observations remain valid in this century. But although many people lived under the same circumstances, why did Arendt foster such an original theory as to define politics only as the humane activities of human beings?

First, Arendt studied German philosophy and deeply committed herself to existentialism and phenomenology. She created the concept of plurality, which is her version of an existential comprehension of human beings. She is concerned with natality rather than with death, in contrast to her teacher Heidegger. She applied a phenomenological approach to politics. Consequently, her phenomenology is not the "phenomenology of consciousness" as proposed by Husserl but a "phenomenology of politics," which means grasping the essence of political phenomena.

Second, Arendt was faithful to her convictions. She maintained integrity throughout her life. The most important task for her was to understand "the burden of our time." She had a talent for combining many materials into a story that is worthy of being read. She also had a good grasp of contemporary history and the history of Western ideas. While she searched for the real meanings of political issues, Arendt was particularly interested in the original meanings of the fundamental terms of politics. She redefined the concepts of politics, power, and freedom. She envisioned the chance to provide a language of politics based on our ordinary lives. This is what she pursued as a brilliant political theorist.

From these perspectives, we can apply her political thinking to analyze political realities ourselves. What we have to learn from her is to construct a better world by reviewing past experiences of humankind and then tackling the political realities of our time. Political theory has the power to turn us in the direction of a better world by examining our way of life.

III

Heinrich Blücher:
A Hidden Source of Hannah Arendt's Political Thought

1. The Man Called "Monsieur"

In considering the development of the political thought of Hannah Arendt, it is important to look at the person of Heinrich Blücher, who first met Arendt in Paris in 1936 and married her four years later. Although many books and several biographies have been written on Arendt since her death in 1975, only in the first and most comprehensive biography, Elisabeth Young-Bruehl's *Hannah Arendt: For Love of the World*, is Blücher's true significance clearly delineated. Since Blücher himself has not left us any published biographical material, the exact contours of Blücher's influence on Arendt have remained obscure. Yet there are several available sources that shed light on the Blücher-Arendt connection: Young-Bruehl's biography, which contains valuable information from interviews with people close to both Arendt and Blücher; Blücher's letters and manuscripts contained in *The Papers of Hannah Arendt* stored at the U.S. Library of Congress in Washington, D.C.; and copies of Blücher's lectures, which are stored in the main library at Bard College in New York State, where Blücher taught for many years. Together, these materials provide a vivid picture of the manner and style of Blücher's influence on Arendt.

Young-Bruehl states in her biography that "Arendt's concern for political action might never have been as deep as it was had she not met and married a very political animal — Heinrich Blücher." [1] Blücher was a former Communist and a man of action, who had participated in the unsuccessful Spartacist rebellion in Germany following the chaos of the early post-World War I period (1918–1919). In contrast to her first husband Günther Stern, who was the son of famous Jewish psychologists and then engaged in his *habilitation* thesis (German academic qualification), Blücher was a largely self-educated German Gentile who had worked as a journalist but had never pursued an academic career. Blücher, Young-Bruehl informs us, [2] was born in Berlin on January 29, 1899, and raised solely by his mother, due to his father's death in a factory accident before his birth. He attended a German *Volksschule* and originally intended to become a public-school teacher. The First World War, however, interrupted his career plans when he was drafted into the army and compelled to fight against the Allied Powers. During the war he spent time in an army hospital recovering from a poison gas attack, a situation that halted his hoped-for advancement to officer status.

In 1918, when the armistice was signed, Blücher returned to Berlin, like many angry and embittered soldiers with leftist leanings, and joined one of the Soldiers' Councils. Blücher participated in the rioting of November 1918, in which leftist revolutionaries proclaimed a new German Republic, and a month later became a member of the newly founded German Communist Party (KPD). In 1919, however, after the failure of street battles and strikes to bring about the anticipated change, Blücher returned to his original career plans by entering a teachers' training program. Blücher did not finish these studies, however, and began to devote his time to working occasionally as a reporter for leftist newspapers. He became a voracious reader during this period, reading books on many topics and attending many lectures at Berlin University and the Hochschule für Politik.

(1) Elisabeth Young-Bruehl, *Hannah Arendt: For Love of the World*, New Haven and London: Yale University Press, 1982, p. xi.

(2) *Ibid.*, pp. 125–127.

When Arendt first met Blücher, she was still married to Stern, although their marriage had clearly soured by this time. According to one of Arendt's friends, Arendt jokingly called Blücher "Monsieur" (3) at a dinner held in her home because he seemed, to her, not so much a Communist as a "bourgeois-in-disguise." With the love having drained out of her first marriage, Arendt and Stern divorced in 1937, and in January 1940, Arendt and Blücher married. The marriage lasted until Blücher's death in 1970, and it appeared to have been a very happy one.

Although Blücher would gradually abandon some of the Communist beliefs he held in his youth, his political activism influenced Arendt profoundly. "With Heinrich Blücher as her teacher, she added to her preliminary reading of Marx, Lenin, and Trotsky a feeling for 'revolutionary *praxis*.' Blücher — not a university man but a proletarian, not a theorist but a man of action, not a Jew but a man for whom thinking was a kind of religion — was Hannah Arendt's New World." (4) Arendt herself, in a letter to Karl Jaspers soon after the Second World War, acknowledged the great impact Blücher had on her thinking. "Thanks to my husband," she wrote to Jaspers, "I have learned to think politically and to see historically." (5)

To be sure, Hannah Arendt had had an interest in the activist and practical side of politics even before she met Blücher. She actively resisted Nazis from the early days of the regime (and indeed was placed under arrest by the Gestapo for her anti-Nazi activities) and worked in Paris to help young Jewish refugees seeking asylum in Palestine. An activist inclination in Arendt seems to have been present from her youth, and a concern with the political and social status of her fellow Jews — what in Europe at the time was called "the Jewish Question" — was what engaged her from a very

---

(3) *Ibid.*, p. 123.

(4) *Ibid.*, p. 124.

(5) Hannah Arendt to Karl Jaspers, January 29, 1946, in *Hannah Arendt/Karl Jaspers Briefwechsel 1926–1969*, hrsg. von Lotte Köhler und Hans Saner, München: Piper, 1985, p. 67.

early period. Despite these early activist leanings, we can say that it was the man Heinrich Blücher who helped to crystallize in Arendt's mind the central importance of actual lived political experience — i.e., of political *praxis* — for understanding the meaning of politics and the nature of political order. Blücher was particularly instrumental in giving Arendt an understanding of workers' councils and the kind of revolutionary *praxis* that had been so alive in the Germany of Blücher's and Arendt's youth.

2. Blücher's Influence on Arendt's Understanding of Totalitarianism

Perhaps nowhere else in Arendt's writing is Blücher's influence more apparent than in *The Origins of Totalitarianism*. Indeed, Arendt dedicated the book to Blücher and once called it "our book," (6) a sign of just how important her continued discussions with her husband (7) had been in shaping her views on totalitarianism.

Totalitarianism as a dynamic movement

The impact of Blücher can be more clearly viewed by comparing Arendt's ideas to an unpublished article by Blücher contained in *Arendt Papers* under the title "Perpetual Motion. Some Tests of the Political Structures of Nazism." Like Arendt, Blücher in the article finds fascism, totalitarianism, and Nazism to be new, unprecedented phenomena, (8) rather than a recurrence of older-style tyrannies. And also, like Arendt, Blücher emphasizes the role of masses and their manipulation by leaders as a key

(6) *Hannah Arendt: For Love of the World*, p. 268.

(7) *Ibid.*, pp. 222–223.

(8) See Heinrich Blücher*, "Perpetual Motion. Some Tests of the Political Structures of Nazism," p. 3, in "Family Papers" of *The Papers of Hannah Arendt*, in the Manuscript Division of the Library of Congress, Washington D.C. (*The author's name is unwritten, but it is presumed to be written by Blücher). In the following, *The Papers of Hannah Arendt* is abridged as *Arendt Papers*.

ingredient in the emergence of totalitarian rule. Blücher also parallels the Arendtian view that Nazism was radically different from any other form of government and the earlier style of German nationalism. On this Blücher writes, "Nazism promised the German people to restore the nation. Actually, Nazism negating political freedom on principle, destroyed the remnants of German nationhood and transformed the German mass society into a military prey horde." (9)

Similarities to Arendt's views can also be seen in Blücher's understanding of Nazism as a dynamic movement in which the terror-prone Gestapo and SS became more and more the driving force of the Nazi party, especially after it took over command of the police. (10) "Nazism," Blücher writes, "bringing forward the mechanism inherent in the isms, changes it into dynamism. In other words, Nazism connects mechanism with a motor that set the machinery of fatalism going." (11) Arendt seems to have been influenced not only by Blücher's view that Nazism was a dynamic political movement but also by the notion that politics at all times was a dynamic and changing process and "to think politically" was to grasp this fact.

Similarities of historical viewpoints

Blücher's influence on Arendt's view of history was perhaps less direct than his influence on her view of totalitarianism, but they both seemed to have shared an aversion to the idea of history as a deterministic process proceeding inexorably through preordained developmental stages, oblivious to the wishes or will of human beings. Blücher seems to have impressed on Arendt the necessity of seeing historical events in their true human uniqueness rather than as the inevitable unfolding of suprahuman forces beyond human control. Arendt herself, in her lecture on "Political Experiences in the Twentieth Century," would come to express sympathy

(9) *Ibid.*, p. 11.
(10) *Ibid.*, p. 22.
(11) *Ibid.*, p. 4.

for the view of Vico that while nature is made by God, history is made by men. (12) While "Adam Smith speaks of the invisible hand, Kant of the Ruse of nature, Hegel of [the] cunning of Reason, all of which work behind men's back[s]," (13) human history for Arendt is made by people and has no preordained telos.

Moreover, historical narrative, as distinct from the actual events of history, is seen by Arendt as a creative, freely willed human activity. Arendt realized that human events become meaningful only when they are subsequently reflected upon and retold as stories. There is, she says, "no history where we can't tell a story. Every sequence of events can be told as a history." (14) Historical narrative requires a storyteller who tells a story, and the storyteller will inevitably select and interpret events from his or her particular point of view. Arendt quotes in this context from Michael Oakeshott who states in his early work, *Experience and its Modes*, that history "is made by nobody save the historian: to write history is the only way of making it." (15) "The story teller never tells everything that happens. He selects, and he selects with a view to the end." (16) This selection, Arendt understood, must be based on some freely chosen value, and to select some value is an act of giving meaning to history. Like the actual events of history, historical narrative is made by people, and the only *telos* it can possibly have is that supplied by the storyteller.

Similarities of views on totalitarianism

Blücher's ideas on totalitarianism run closely parallel to those of Arendt, though it is difficult to say exactly who influenced whom. It is probably safe

(12) See Hannah Arendt, "Political Experiences in the Twentieth Century," lectures, Cornell University, 1965, in *Arendt Papers*, p. 023761.

(13) *Ibid.*, p. 023761.

(14) *Ibid.*, p. 023761.

(15) *Ibid.*, p. 023761 (quoted from Michael Oakeshott, *Experience and Its Modes*, London: The Cambridge University Press, 1933, p. 99).

(16) *Ibid.*, p. 023762.

to assume that their understanding of totalitarianism — and particularly of Nazism — was commonly forged in their continuing dialogue of many years, in which each functioned as a sounding board for the other. Like Arendt, but unlike many other leftist intellectuals, Blücher tended to equate Nazi-style totalitarianism with Bolshevik-style Stalinism. Although Blücher in his writings says comparatively little about the Soviet political regime, he does at one point refer to the "totalitarian government-form of the Bolshevik mold," (17) clearly implying the distance he preferred to keep from orthodox Marxist-Leninist defenders of Soviet communism.

A second parallel with Arendt's view on totalitarianism can be seen in Blücher's emphasis on the central importance of racism in Nazi ideology. Racist thinking, according to Blücher, was just what Nazism needed to harness nationalism for supranational ends. "Within Germany Nazis needed only the Jews as spectral enemies, while South African Nazis could also use the colored — neither of them, however, had any use for Freemasons and Jesuits." (18) Like Arendt, Blücher saw racism as a defining feature of Nazism and what distinguished it from Italian fascism and other types of extreme nationalism.

A third parallel between Blücher's views and those of Arendt is his understanding of totalitarianism as an attempt to overcome Western man's sense of isolated, fractured existence through the deliberate abandonment of the individual's personality and will to power of a mass movement. "Why," Blücher asked in one of his lectures at Bard College, "can specialists so easily be won to totalitarianism?" (19) He answered himself: "Because they lost their freedom, feel isolated in their specialty and long for unification." (20)

(17) Heinrich Blücher, "Nationalsozialismus und Neonationalismus," p. 1, in *Arendt Papers*.

(18) *Ibid.*, pp. 3–4.

(19) Heinrich Blücher, "The Common Core Course," p. 8, Introduction to the Common Course, delivered on November 16, 1952, and stored at Bard College Library, Annandale-on-Hudson.

(20) *Ibid.*, p. 8.

Blücher stressed in his lectures the difference between truly free education, which sought to open creative possibilities in the student, and totalitarian education, which sought to enslave the human mind by suppressing free inquiry. "The natural inquisitiveness of the mind," he noted, "... is suppressed by totalitarian education which tends to transform man into an altogether conditioned being; as it must be strengthened by our own education." (21) By contrast, the goal of our own education, he said, must be to strengthen this natural inquisitiveness. Each of these ideas has parallels in Arendt's thought.

3. The Anti-authoritarian Personality

For Arendt, Blücher was both a partner in their common enterprise of free thought as well as someone who shared her own aversion to authoritarianism. Blücher was even more of an egalitarian than Arendt, since he did not, as she tended to do, limit the principle of equality to the political realm. Blücher was in fact something of a proto-feminist: He emphasized the fundamental equality of men and women and insisted that every other form of inequality was anchored in this basic difference. (22) Jesus, he says, established the equality of all human beings, and to this end He had first to abolish the inequality between man and woman.

Characteristics of Blücher's anti-authoritarianism

Blücher's anti-authoritarianism extended to his position as professor at Bard College. (23) One former Bard student, Jack Blum, remembers how Blücher was once asked by a student in his class how he would like to be addressed, whether as professor or doctor: "He looked at the student with

(21) *Ibid.*, pp. 8–9.

(22) See Heinrich Blücher, "Jesus of Nazareth," Lecture I, p. 28, delivered at New School for Social Research, May 21, 1954, and stored at Bard College Library.

(23) After assuming a number of jobs following his migration to America, including that of research assistant and factory worker, Blücher became a teacher at Bard, a small college in Annandale-on-Hudson in the state of New York.

mock anger and said, 'My friend, my name is Heinrich Bluecher[Blücher], and I wish to be known by my name. I insist that each of you recognize me as a person and address me by my name and nothing more.'"[24]

Blücher taught Bard college freshmen in what was known as the Common Course curriculum, a Great Books-type program that was created by Bard's president, James Case. Case once remarked that he "thought he had found in Blücher just what he wanted, 'a Socratic man.'"[25] The library of Bard College holds copies of tape recordings of Blücher's lectures, which he gave at both Bard College and at the New School for Social Research in Manhattan. This Common Course curriculum at Bard took up a wide variety of thinkers from throughout recorded history. Young-Bruehl remarked that Blücher's lectures were "designed to introduce students to the sources of creative power, and for this purpose he selected a number of 'great thinkers' who had, he felt, discovered human creative capacities not known before them, a diverse group that included Abraham, Jesus, Zarathustra, Buddha, Lao-tse, Homer, Heraclitus, and Socrates, the 'arch-fathers of the free personality.'"[26] These great ancient thinkers, together with a number of modern thinkers such as Kierkegaard, were seen to exemplify "the creative powers of man."[27] Blücher was said to have had a powerful influence in provoking his own students to think about the wisdom of the past, and he became something of a cult figure among Bard students.

Blücher's lectures were not restricted to any one style or school of philosophy but continued a pattern of inquiry into the received wisdom of the past in the manner of Socrates. As Karl Jaspers once wrote to Arendt, Blücher was "an identical twin of Socrates"[28] — or as former

(24) Jack Blum, "Heinrich Bleucher 1899–1970" (a memorial article), *St. Stephen's Alumni Magazine*, November 1970, p. 10.

(25) *Hannah Arendt: For Love of the World*, p. 269.

(26) *Ibid.*, p. 270.

(27) "The Common Core Course," p. 1.

(28) Karl Jaspers to Hannah Arendt, November 2, 1963, in *Hannah Arendt/Karl Jaspers Briefwechsel*, p. 566.

student Jack Blum phrased it, he taught philosophy "by being a philosopher, by continuously questioning and testing the 'wisdom' dished up by our society." (29) His interest in Socratic inquiry, Greek philosophy, as well as political and intellectual freedom obviously had close parallels with Arendt's interests (though unlike Blücher, Arendt never displayed any interest in Indian or Chinese thought).

Jaspers suggested that Blücher was a hidden source of Arendt's political thought, when he stated in a letter to Arendt, "As Plato's thoughts did not become what they were without Socrates, so your thoughts have not become what they are without Blücher." (30) Arendt, of course, was influenced by many thinkers, including existentialists like Nietzsche, Heidegger and Jaspers, as well as many others in the European intellectual tradition. Her thinking, however, was not merely derivative but occurred as an ongoing process of philosophical inquiry and dialogue — a "living thought" that she developed not merely by reading books but also by reflecting on her political experiences during the Nazi period and the ongoing dialogue with her husband Heinrich Blücher that filled almost the entire second half of her life.

How to distinguish Socrates from Plato

Of considerable significance is the fact that both Blücher and Arendt distinguished Socrates from Plato and attempted to de-Platonize Socrates. This is of decisive importance in determining the intellectual tradition from which both emerged. Blücher and Arendt were both in some sense children of the Enlightenment whose concern with critical reason precluded a concern with mystical thought. Like Arendt, Blücher had the highest regard for the de-Platonized Socrates (whom he believed to be the historical Socrates) as well as for the rationalist Immanuel Kant, and the thinkers he discussed in his lectures were entirely non-mystical.

---

(29) Jack Blum, "Heinrich Blücher 1899–1970," p. 9.

(30) Karl Jaspers to Hannah Arendt, December 10, 1965, in *Hannah Arendt/Karl Jaspers Briefwechsel*, p. 652.

Blücher was not only a Socratic man but also a thinker who respected Socrates and tried to learn from his life-long quest. The title of one of Blücher's Common Course lectures was "Socrates," and in other lectures Socrates and pre-Socratic philosophers are often mentioned. Although Blücher recognized the difficulty of distinguishing the thoughts of Socrates from the thoughts of Plato — "the thoughts of Socrates," he says, "are so mixed with the thoughts of Plato that it has always been a hard task to distinguish them" (31) — he insisted on the necessity of doing this and was particularly insistent on distinguishing the mystical and other-worldly Plato from the distinctly non-mystical, this-worldly Socrates. In the latter context he quotes from Aristotle: "Socrates himself never talked about ideas" (*Metaphysics*, 987b). (32)

Although "Plato loved Socrates," (33) Blücher sees the two philosophers as representing two entirely different lines of development in Greek philosophical thought. Whereas Socrates for Blücher was thoroughly non-mystical and, like the pre-Socratic Heraclitus, free from superstition and the mental framework of myth, Plato, he believed, was a mystic philosopher in the tradition of Pythagoras and his school. Crossing the line drawn by Socrates, Plato, he says, uses myth and "designs not only a possible hereafter but also the exact indication of it as a kind of punishment and reward." (34) Yet "to talk about things after death is entirely non-Heraclitean and non-Socratic," (35) Blücher contended.

This fundamental Socratic/Platonic difference, Blücher believed, is also reflected in the two philosophers' differing views of knowledge. For Plato, Blücher explains, knowledge is attained by a very special kind of philosopher, "somebody who had hidden knowledge, somebody who can attain knowledge

(31) Heinrich Blücher, "Socrates," Lecture I, April 30, 1954, p. 4. Two Lectures at New School for Social Research, stored at Bard College Library.

(32) *Ibid.*, p. 4.

(33) *Ibid.*, p. 5.

(34) *Ibid.*, p. 7 (underlined by Blücher).

(35) *Ibid.*, p. 7.

other human beings cannot attain." [36] Philosophers are clearly placed above people in the marketplace. By contrast, "Socrates," Blücher said, "talked with everyone." [37] "Socrates was of the opinion that everybody was capable of reasoning and therefore that everyone can and should philosophize in order to attain freedom." [38] Socrates, moreover, founded no school of philosophy in the manner of Pythagoras, Plato and Aristotle. [39] He was more at home, rather, talking to everyday Athenians, seeking contradictions in their ideas and discourse. For Socrates, Blücher says, philosophy is "the capability of free judgment through the use of reason," [40] and this capacity, he believed, was the common possession of everyone, not just an unusually gifted elite.

Blücher specifically criticized the Platonic belief in the possibility of attaining a kind of transcendental unity with divine ideas. Human beings, Blücher holds, should use the faculty of thinking that is commonly given, but human judgment and human wisdom, he believes, cannot match absolute wisdom. "As Socrates realized, the absolute wisdom and judgment can never be reached. We have no divine judgment. We have no divine qualities. We have no divine logic. We have no divine will. We have only, as Zarathustra said, a human will, but we are not Ahuramazda. We do not, in Lao-Tze's terms, have divine unity with the Tao." [41] It was Blücher's view, in other words, that human beings cannot transcend themselves. To transcend oneself means to unite with God, and this is not possible according to Blücher. For this reason, he challenged Plato's belief that it is possible for philosophers to attain knowledge of divine ideas, and he said that "Plato's idea that philosophers should be kings is something that would never have entered Socrates' mind." [42]

---

(36) *Ibid.*, p. 8.
(37) *Ibid.*, p. 8.
(38) *Ibid.*, p. 8 (underlined by Blücher).
(39) *Ibid.*, pp. 8–9.
(40) *Ibid.*, p. 10.
(41) *Ibid.*, p. 14 (underlined by Blücher).
(42) *Ibid.*, p. 6.

According to Blücher, the abyss between the human and the divine is absolute, and one can never cross it. "If we could transcend our human qualities," Blücher contends, "then we would be able to enter the realm of the highest being and that means we would be able to unite with God, but we do not have that possibility." (43)

Like Blücher, Arendt distinguishes Socrates and Plato and places the former in the category of non-mystical philosophers. In *Thinking*, the first volume of *The Life of the Mind*, she connects Socrates and Kant and clarifies qualities of critical thinking. Unlike Plato, Socrates, Arendt points out, never believed thinking to be a privileged capability of the few and never limited objects of thinking to those that could be perceived only by intellectually superior men. Intellectually superior men, Arendt insists, are not necessarily morally superior men. She criticizes in this context Plato's penchant for "noble natures." (44)

In her *Lectures on Kant's Political Philosophy*, Arendt distinguishes Socrates and Plato and points out that the critical thinking of Socrates embodies the method of questions and answers in which one's thinking is examined by others. "According to Plato," Arendt writes, "he [Socrates] did this by the art of *krinein*, of sorting out and separating and distinguishing (*technē diakritikē*, the art of discrimination). According to Plato (but not according to Socrates), the result is 'the purification of the soul from conceits that stand in the way of knowledge.'" (45) Arendt thus distinguishes Plato and Socrates quite sharply, and sees Plato alone concerned with "the purification of the soul." (46) Arendt also stresses the fact that Socrates belonged to no school and founded no school, which is similarly stressed by Blücher. Critical thought for Arendt involves continual criticism and examination, and it is

(43) *Ibid.*, p. 17.
(44) Hannah Arendt, *The Life of the Mind*, vol. 1: *Thinking*, New York: Harcourt Brace Jovanovich, 1978, p. 180.
(45) Hannah Arendt, *Lectures on Kant's Political Philosophy*, ed. by Ronald Beiner, Sussex: The Harvester Press, 1982, p. 37.
(46) *Ibid.*, p. 37.

open to everyone who will engage in the process. It has nothing to do with esoteric doctrines that are hidden from all but a small group of men. Nor is it an activity that depends on the revered doctrines of the founder of a school. All "the schools and sects," according to Arendt, "are unenlightened (in Kantian parlance) because they depend on the doctrines of their founders." (47) Arendt sees herself standing in the tradition of critical thought represented by Socrates and Kant, a tradition that she believes is by its nature anti-authoritarian.

Similarity of views on human faculties

There are many more parallels that can be drawn between Arendt's thought and that of Blücher. Both, for instance, placed a high value on the role of communication in human affairs, both stressed the importance of imagining oneself in the position of the other (48) as a means of furthering the processes of interpersonal communication and critical thought, and both stressed the importance of the phenomenon of human birth. The last point of agreement is particularly important. Blücher says in his lecture on "Jesus of Nazareth" that "the birth of a human being is the most significant fact in man's world." (49) The nativity of Jesus, he says, is a story of a human being who was born in a stable and found naked in a manger without social status. "The hope in man and in every man's birth is discovered here," Blücher said, "Every child born into the world is an infinite hope for mankind." (50) Arendt also stressed the miracle of birth. Man himself, according to her, is always a new beginning and holds the possibility of causing an event that could not be predicted earlier. "Action," she writes, "is in fact, the miracle-working

---

(47) *Ibid.*, p. 38.

(48) Blücher emphasized that "I am an I and a possible You in myself. If I weren't I could not even think. This possible existence is a precondition for thinking." "Socrates," Lecture I, p. 25 (underlined by Blücher).

(49) "Jesus of Nazareth," Lecture I, p. 11 (underlined by Blücher), New School for Social Research, May 14, 1954, stored at Bard College Library.

(50) *Ibid.*, p. 11.

faculty of man, as Jesus of Nazareth, whose insights into this faculty can be compared in their originality and unprecedentedness with Socrates' insights into the possibility of thought, must have known very well when he linked the power to forgive to the more general power of performing miracles, putting both on the same level and within the reach of man." (51)

Blücher, of course, was not the only person with whom Arendt conversed or the only one who influenced the development of her thought. But his influence was very great, especially in regard to her attitudes toward authoritarianism and egalitarianism. Her book, *On Revolution*, which Blücher once described as her "best book," (52) brilliantly narrates the political significance of freedom that Arendt had learned both from her own experience and, perhaps even more so, from that of Blücher. Blücher was her intimate intellectual companion throughout most of the latter years of her life, and his conversations and understanding, even over such difficult matters as the vicious attacks launched against Arendt's book on Eichmann, were of inestimable value to her.

4. Heidegger vs. Blücher

It is interesting to consider the question of who was more influential on Arendt's thinking, Heidegger or Blücher. While much has been written of Arendt's relation to the former, little has been written of the Arendt-Blücher connection, despite the fact that there is reason to believe that Blücher was much more important to her intellectual development than was Heidegger.

Arendt's relationship to Heidegger

According to Elźbieta Ettinger, Arendt fell in love with Heidegger

(51) Hannah Arendt, *The Human Condition*, Chicago: University of Chicago Press, 1958, pp. 246–247.

(52) Heinrich Blücher to Hannah Arendt, March 4, 1963, in *Hannah Arendt/Heinrich Blücher Briefe 1936–1968*, hrsg. von Lotte Köhler, 1996, p. 559.

at the tender age of 18 when she was a student in his philosophy class at the University of Marburg. Ettinger was able to gain permission from Heidegger's son to view the correspondence between Heidegger and Arendt, which had been closed to the public out of respect for the feelings of Heidegger's wife Elfriede, who died in 1992. Ettinger divides Arendt's relationship with Heidegger into three phases: the first, from 1925 to roughly 1930, when the two were lovers; the second, from the early 1930s until 1950 when their relationship was radically changed by Heidegger's joining the Nazi Party; and the third, from 1950 until Arendt's death in 1975, when the two resumed their old relationship and built a new one.[(53)] Ettinger's book was sensational because it suggested that Arendt consistently defended Heidegger against those who charged him with Nazi collaboration out of a renewed emotional attachment to the philosopher that followed in the wake of their 1950 meeting in post-war Freiburg.

Arendt certainly displayed hostility toward Heidegger in her earlier 1946 essay "What Is Existenz Philosophy?" In that essay, Arendt criticized Heidegger for his Nazi past and positioned his thought in the line of German Romanticism, a tradition that led to Nazism: "Heidegger is, in fact, the last (we hope) romantic — as it were, a tremendously gifted Friedrich Schlegel or Adam Mueller, whose complete irresponsibility was attributed partly to the delusion of genius, partly to desperation."[(54)] In a letter to Karl Jaspers written in the same year, she went so far as to call Heidegger "a potential murderer."[(55)] In the late 1940s, however, Arendt's attitude toward Heidegger began to change, though it is doubtful whether this change was due primarily to emotional factors as Ettinger suggests. Rather, it was during this period

---

(53) See Elźbieta Ettinger, *Hannah Arendt·Martin Heidegger*, New Haven and London: Yale University Press, 1995, p. 2.

(54) Hannah Arendt, "What Is Existenz Philosophy?" *Partisan Review*, vol. 13, no. 1 (Winter 1946), p. 46 (quoted from the footnote on the page).

(55) Hannah Arendt to Karl Jaspers, July 9, 1946, in *Hannah Arendt/Karl Jaspers Briefwechsel*, p. 84.

that Arendt read Heidegger's lectures on Nietzsche and Heraclitus, [56] which convinced her that Heidegger was no Nazi and certainly no anti-Semite. Contrary to the impression created by Ettinger's work, Arendt seems to have changed her negative view of Heidegger, which she held during the thirties and early forties, sometime before she actually met him again in Freiburg in 1950.

Concerning Heidegger's much-criticized address upon assuming the office of Rector of Freiburg University, Arendt wrote that she doubted "that Heidegger at that time had any clear notion of what Nazism was all about. But he learned quickly, and after about eight or ten months, his whole 'political past' was over." [57] Such an *apologia* will strike many as utterly feeble, since Heidegger's commitment to the Nazi Party was more than a short-term affair — indeed, he kept up his party membership until 1945. Arendt, however, was certain that Heidegger was not anti-Semitic, and she was convinced of "the philosophical relevance of Heidegger's analyses" [58] to understanding the modern predicament. She considered it her task to communicate aspects of his philosophy to people in the United States, and she was able to overlook in this context certain negative aspects of his personal and political life.

How Blücher stands in comparison with Heidegger

In comparison with Heidegger, Blücher was more open-minded and generous to Arendt. Blücher, Ettinger writes, "was warm but not sentimental, wise but not overpowering or patronizing, respectful of Arendt's

---

(56) Hannah Arendt To Dr. Faber, November 1, 1960, in *Arendt Papers*, p. 005965. By 1949, Arendt probably had access to a private manuscript of Heidegger's Nietzsche lectures (see *Hannah Arendt/Karl Jaspers Briefwechsel*, pp. 178, 751).

(57) Hannah Arendt to Dr. Faber, November 1, 1960, in *Arendt Papers*, p. 005964. Arendt writes that "Were you ever a member of this or that party? Which, properly or improperly are included in the questionnaires of the police?" (*Ibid.*, pp. 005964–005965).

(58) Hannah Arendt, *Men in Dark Times*, New York: Harcourt, Brace & World, INC, 1968, p. ix .

mind and independence, caring but not possessive or domineering." [59] This attitude lasted until his death in 1970. Blücher's importance to Arendt is perhaps well characterized by the question she posed to her friends on the night following his death: "How am I to live now?" [60] Blücher had been a great inspiration for her political development as well as her intimate partner in dialogue, and his death was something very painful for her to contemplate.

Heidegger, by contrast, was cool and stand-offish. *The Human Condition* — which many consider her greatest work — is not dedicated to anyone, in contrast to Arendt's other works (her early work, *Rahel Varnhagen*, is dedicated to Anne Weil, her lifelong Jewish friend and a descendant of Moses Mendelssohn; *The Origins of Totalitarianism* and *Between Past and Future* are dedicated to Blücher; *On Revolution* is dedicated to Gertrud and Karl Jaspers; *Crises of the Republic* is dedicated to Mary McCarthy; and her essay "Thinking and Moral Considerations: A Lecture" is dedicated to W. H. Auden). Nevertheless, Arendt wanted to dedicate *The Human Condition* to Heidegger because, as she would write to him, "The book evolved directly from the first Marburg days and it owes you just about everything in every regard." [61] However, when the German version of the book, *Vita activa oder vom tätigen Leben*, was sent to him along with the letter containing the above acknowledgement of his contribution, he treated it coolly and sent her no opinion of the book. [62] Heidegger probably could not understand the significance of her phenomenological thinking on action and politics. Although Arendt owed much to Heidegger in terms of her thinking on human affairs, it is evident that she was writing on a level altogether different from that of Heidegger. Arendt had moved beyond Heidegger's preoccupation with the

---

(59) *Hannah Arendt·Martin Heidegger*, p. 40.

(60) Hannah Arendt/Mary McCarthy, *Between Friends: The Correspondence of Hannah Arendt and Mary McCarthy, 1949–1975*, ed. by Carol Brightman, New York: Harcourt Brace & Company, 1995, p. 266.

(61) Hannah Arendt to Martin Heidegger, October 28, 1960, in *Hannah Arendt·Martin Heidegger*, p. 114.

(62) *Ibid.*, pp. 114–116.

self-centered *Da-sein* to an evaluation of human existence in the world of human activity.

The world of politics is the world in which both Blücher and Arendt lived during the Nazi period. As previously mentioned, Blücher believed *On Revolution* to be her best book, since it showed the positive side of political action and is also a great narrative describing the glory and misery of the people who participated in the process of modern and contemporary revolutions. When she was accused of having exculpated Eichmann in her book on the Eichmann trial, Blücher correctly understood the book and the absurdity of the accusations leveled against her.

The parallels between the thoughts of Blücher and Arendt can be attributed to the intimate, ongoing nature of the intellectual dialogue they pursued over a period of more than thirty years. Arendt was fortunate to find in her husband the best person to understand her work, and Blücher may be viewed as the hidden source and inspiration of Arendt's key ideas. What should be understood is that it was not only to Blücher that Arendt showed enduring loyalty. She was always loyal to her friends. Her concern for people could be clearly seen in her habit of always responding personally to letters from readers of her works, which is a sign of her love for the world.

Arendt's relationship with Heinrich Blücher was clearly the most important one of her life. It was an ongoing, two-way dialogue in which neither was dominant and from which both richly profited. Arendt's relationship with Heidegger, however, was very different. It lacked the egalitarian reciprocity of the Blücher-Arendt relationship and, in the end, it would cool under Heidegger's self-aloof arrogance. It was Blücher who enabled Arendt to break the early spell Heidegger had cast over her and to free her to chart her own independent journey on the sea of political thinking.

IV

The Relevance of Hannah Arendt's Reflections on Civil Disobedience

1. Introduction

Civil disobedience is defined as a public act that disobeys an unjust law or policy with the full knowledge and acceptance of the fact that the disobedience will lead to punishment. Civil disobedience can be performed individually or in concert with others, but to be considered civil disobedience it must be done publicly (not secretly or in private) and it must be nonviolent. Under democratic regimes, acts of civil disobedience do not aim to change or damage the constitutional system, but to change specific unjust laws or policies. Under such circumstances, those who disobey unjust laws respect the constitutional order and do not intend to overthrow the political system itself. However, under tyrannical dictatorships or oppressive colonial regimes the entire existing political order can be a target of mass civil disobedience. This "complete civil disobedience," as Mohandas K. Gandhi called it, (1) is significantly different from the type of civil disobedience that occurs in constitutional democracies.

---

(1) Mohandas K. Gandhi, "Civil Disobedience" (*Young India*, August 4, 1921), in *The Collected Works of Mahatma Gandhi*, vol. 24, New Delhi: Publications Division, Ministry of Information and Broadcasting, Government of India, 3rd revised edition, 2000 [1967]. p. 47.

In this article, I focus on the concept of civil disobedience rather than the related idea of civil resistance. The latter involves collective actions that may deny the legitimacy of an existing regime and may also include the use of violence. John Locke, in his *Two Treatises of Government*, asserted that people, under certain circumstances, have the right to change the form of government under which they live — even if it requires the use of violence. Locke further adds that he "*who may resist, must be allowed to strike.*" (2) Since the word "resistance" itself implies for some people the idea of force or violence, when nonviolent means of protest became popular in some quarters during the 19th century, the words "nonviolent resistance" or "passive resistance" were used by the people who wanted to preclude violent action from their means of protest. According to Michael Randle, nonviolent forms of collective action such as boycotts and strikes began to evolve in the 19th century. (3) It was also in this century that the more elaborate theories of civil disobedience were first elaborated, with Henry David Thoreau being the first to coin the actual term "civil disobedience."

Paradigmatic examples of nonviolent civil disobedience would be displayed by Thoreau in the first half of the 19th century, between the 1890s and 1940s by Mohandas K. Gandhi in South Africa and India, and in the mid-20th century by Martin Luther King, Jr. in America. King patterned his nonviolent protests after the earlier Gandhian movement, adding some distinct elements of his own.

Hannah Arendt first experienced civil disobedience movements in the 1950s and 1960s in her adopted country, America. Although she was neither an advocate of civil disobedience nor a theorist of nonviolent action, she published an important essay on the subject in 1970, entitled simply "Civil

---

(2) John Locke, *Two Treatises of Government*, critical edition with an introduction by Peter Laslett, 2nd edition, reprinted with amendments, Cambridge: Cambridge University Press, 1970, p. 439 (emphasis in original).

(3) See Michael Randle, *Civil Resistance*, London: Fontana Press, 1994, pp. 19–51.

Disobedience,"[4] and reprinted it as one of the four chapters in her book *Crises of the Republic* (1972). This latter work is unique among her writings as it deals almost exclusively with contemporary political controversies and current affairs. The civil rights and anti-Vietnam War movements of the 1960s in America form the background of this book. Although the topic that she chose was contemporary, she approached the imminent issues from a historical and theoretical perspective that lent to her reflections a depth of insight and an enduring value that command our attention even today.

In this article, I focus on Arendt's reflections on civil disobedience because they continue to shed light on many important issues in contemporary political theory, including political obligation, consent of the governed, and the rights of conscience. In addition, I consider the subsequent development of her political thinking as it relates to the issues raised in her 1972 book. Since I contend that civil disobedience can be an important element in the strengthening of democracy "from below" — that is, through the voluntary actions of ordinary citizens — I believe that it is important to recapture some of Arendt's critical insights.

2. Arendt's View of Civil Disobedience

Arendt wrote on civil disobedience because, similar to many other thinkers, she believed it was an important component in any treatment of judicial problems. In a similar vein, John Rawls, one of the leading political philosophers of the 20th century, addressed civil disobedience in his most important work, *A Theory of Justice* (1971).[5] The appearance of mass movements of civil disobedience during the 20th century provided political

---

(4) Hannah Arendt, "Civil Disobedience," *The New Yorker*, September 12, 1970, pp. 70–105; reprinted in *Crises of the Republic*, New York: Harcourt Brace Jovanovich, 1972.

(5) See John Rawls, *A Theory of Justice*, Cambridge, Massachusetts: Belknap Press of Harvard University Press, 1971, pp. 363–391.

thinkers such as Rawls and Arendt important reasons to reflect on how such movements concern an overall understanding of the nature of justice in both law and politics.

The concept of civil disobedience

According to political scientist Carl Cohen, who wrote many articles on this topic in the 1960s, an act of civil disobedience is characterized by four features. Civil disobedience is (1) "an act that breaks law"; (2) it "must be a *public* act"; (3) it "must be more than illegal and public — it must be an act of protest"; and (4) "it must be *nonviolent*." [(6)] Reflections by American thinkers about civil disobedience became particularly salient in the 1960s because of the public impact of both the nonviolent civil rights movement and the widespread protests against the Vietnam War (the latter being usually, but not always, nonviolent). Issues of both ethics and political theory were raised as many ordinary citizens were forced to confront the problem of whether to obey a law or policy that opposed one's conscience. The protest movements in America at this time rarely called into question the legitimacy of the American constitutional order. Rather, they were focused on very specific laws or policies — such as the segregation laws in the American South or the Selective Service Act, which required some young men to serve in the Vietnam War — that the protesters deemed immoral and contrary to the dictates of a well-formed conscience.

Arendt's arguments on civil disobedience clearly reflect the political realities and controversies in America during this period. But, as previously stated, she approaches these issues from a broad historical and theoretical perspective that returns to Thoreau in Concord (Massachusetts) and Socrates in Athens (Greece). Arendt believed that these two thinkers are of paradigmatic importance in our perception of the legitimacy of civil disobedience. One crucial common point that she found in both thinkers was

---

(6) See Carl Cohen, "Essence and Ethics of Civil Disobedience," *Nation*, No. 198 (March 16, 1964), pp. 257–258 (emphasis in original).

the belief that the civilly disobedient, in addition to being nonviolent, must be willing to go to jail or otherwise face the legal punishments involved in their disobedience. Few, Arendt writes, would disagree with the statement of American Senator Philip A. Hart that "any tolerance that I might feel toward punishment of the disobeyer is dependent on his willingness to accept whatever punishment the law might impose." (7) Such a view evokes the popular understanding — or misunderstanding — of Socrates and his trial before the Athenian court.

But, Arendt herself could not entirely endorse such a view, especially in the context of America and its system of constitutional law, which encourages test cases in which people deliberately disobey laws to test their constitutionality and ultimate legitimacy. Arendt clearly opposes the common understanding that acts of civil disobedience must always be accompanied by an eagerness to go to jail or to accept punishment for violating a law. She quotes in this context from the legal writer Harrop A. Freeman: "No lawyer goes into court and says, 'Your Honor, this man wants to be punished.'" (8) According to Arendt, self-sacrifice should not be demanded of the disobedient.

Arendt also opposes the popular view that would narrow the concept of civil disobedience to include only protest actions performed within the context of broader acceptance of the basic structure of the existing regime. She asks rhetorically, "Did Gandhi accept the 'frame of established authority,' which was British rule in India? Did he respect the 'general legitimacy of the system of laws' in the colony?" (9) The obvious answer to both questions is "no," yet the Indian protest movement led by Gandhi was paradigmatic for Arendt, as for most writers in mid-20th-century America, of nonviolent civil disobedience. Civil disobedience might acquire different forms, Arendt

---

(7) "Civil Disobedience," in *Crises of the Republic*, p. 52.

(8) *Ibid.*, p. 54; the quotation is from the special issue of the *Rutgers Law Review* (vol. 21, Fall 1966) on "Civil Disobedience and the Law," p. 26.

(9) *Ibid.*, p. 77.

believed, depending on the context of the political order in which it was employed. In the case of Gandhi's India, the actions of civil disobedience sought "drastic" changes that included the most basic question of who should govern India — the Indians or the British.

In the 1960s America, civil disobedience movements did not need to question the basic structure of the government. In the movement to abolish racial segregation in the Deep South, the protesters had merely to appeal to the equal protection guarantees of the American Constitution and to the ideal of universal, God-given human rights that almost all Americans accepted and that had been proclaimed in the most exalted terms in the American Declaration of Independence. Opposition to the Vietnam War could similarly occur within the existing structure of government and pattern of understanding about the legitimacy of official decisions to wage war. The anti-war protesters of the 1960s objected to the fact that the war in Vietnam was launched without any formal declaration of war by the American Congress — a clear violation of a very explicit constitutional imperative. Moreover, many would argue that, even if there had been a formal declaration of war, such a war would not have been justifiable, since the Vietnamese were fighting a legitimate anti-colonial war just as the Americans had done in their own revolution against the British Empire.

Since the 1960s, the concept of civil disobedience has expanded in scope from how it was previously understood. In addition to laws considered gravely unjust or immoral, sometimes morally neutral laws of a largely regulatory character are disobeyed as a means of changing government policy. [10] But, while the periphery can be expanded, there remains at the core of civil disobedience, whether in its earlier or expanded version, the belief in the propriety of refusing to obey laws deemed unjust or immoral by one's conscience.

---

(10) See Gene Sharp, *There Are Realistic Alternatives*, Boston: The Albert Einstein Institution, 2003, p. 32.

Civil disobedience and the creation of power

While the question of conscience remains important for Arendt, more important for her is the political dimension of civil disobedience. In her essay, Arendt tends to identify such activity with minority groups, stating that minorities, who are united more by common moral convictions than by common interests, feel they must take a stand against government policies "even if they have reason to assume that these policies are backed by a majority." [11] Arendt clearly distinguishes political power — which in another important article, "On Violence," she identifies with majority support in democratic countries — from justice or conformity with moral principles. Analogous to Alexis de Tocqueville and John Stuart Mill, she was well aware that majorities in democratic countries can rule unjustly. One of the benefits of civil disobedience, she believed, is that even small, oppressed minorities can use this tactic to win the sympathy of a much larger audience while remaining nonviolent.

Arendt recognizes that the idea of consent has a long tradition within the American political order. The idea that legitimate government depends on the consent of the governed, and that those who do the governing have a contractual obligation to rule justly over those whom they govern, is enshrined in both of America's founding documents: The Declaration of Independence and the American Constitution. Arendt points out that the American ideas of contract and consent stemmed not only from John Locke but also from the Mayflower Compact dating back to the earliest English settlers. The point is that the creation of political society by social contract "from the Mayflower Compact to the establishment of the thirteen colonies" in the 17th and 18th centuries was "no mere a fiction" but an entity. [12] The settlers combined into a body politic by mutual consent and decided to maintain their power by consent "not in the very old sense of mere acquiescence, with its distinction between rule over willing subjects and rule

(11) "Civil Disobedience," p. 56.
(12) *Ibid.*, p. 85.

over the unwilling ones, but in the sense of active support and continuing participation in all matters of public interest."[13] Important historical experiences in America reinforce this English idea of contract and consent — indeed, the American system of government was specifically designed, through a system of federalism, checks and balances, and dispersed power, to maintain the proper relationship between the government and the people. (Ideas of hierarchical subordination made famous in the political philosophy of Thomas Hobbes and the divine right of kings were anathema to almost all Americans.) More important to the maintenance of freedom and just government than even these structural features of American government, Arendt believed, was a healthy democratic political culture that fosters a sense of citizen responsibility — including a willingness to reject unjust laws and policies.

In general, it is more preferable to oppose the course of government action by legal rather than illegal means, but there are times when people's lives and freedoms are so egregiously threatened by government oppression, or when legal methods require so long a time period to execute (during which the oppression would continue), that such methods can be legitimately abandoned for the tactics of civil disobedience. Under such circumstances, the oppressed can justifiably organize themselves in nonviolent protest movements that, through their civil disobedience, seek to alter the current power relations by gaining support among a wider public. The American tradition of consent involves the idea that government must be based on a mutual agreement of the people, who have a right to decide what policies of its government are right or just. It is the people, coming together in mutual association, who decide whether a given policy should be accepted or rejected. As Arendt writes: "Consent and the right to dissent became the inspiring and organizing principles of action that taught the inhabitants of this continent [i.e., North America] the 'art of associating together,' from

---

(13) *Ibid.*, p. 85.

which sprang those voluntary associations whose role Tocqueville was the first to notice, with amazement, admiration, and some misgiving; he thought them the peculiar strength of the American political system." (14)

According to Arendt, this aspect of American political culture, which stresses the importance of voluntary associations, had sustained the tradition of civic participation and political freedom. This tradition required a public space where citizens could speak and act freely. She quotes from Tocqueville's *Democracy in America*: "As soon as several inhabitants of the United States have taken up an opinion or a feeling which they wish to promote in the world, [or have found some fault they wish to correct], they look out for mutual assistance, and as soon as they have found one another out, they combine. *From that moment, they are no longer isolated men but a power seen from afar*, whose actions serve for an example and whose language is listened to." (15)

Arendt observed a connection between the civil disobedience movements that she had witnessed in America in the 1950s and 1960s and the American penchant for voluntary associations described by Tocqueville in the 1830s. "It is my contention," she writes, "that civil disobedients are nothing but the latest form of voluntary association, and that they are thus in tune with the oldest tradition of the country." (16) According to her, voluntary associations are not political parties but "ad-hoc organizations that pursue short-term goals and disappear when the goal has been reached. Only in the case of their prolonged failure and of an aim of great importance may they 'constitute, as it were, a separate nation in the midst of the nation, a government within the government.'" (17) This type of citizen-based activism involves the horizontal concept of power that Arendt articulates in *The Human Condition*

(14) *Ibid.*, p. 94.
(15) *Ibid.*, p. 95 (quoted from Tocqueville, *Democracy in America*, vol. 2, book 2, chap. 5; emphasis by Arendt).
(16) *Ibid.*, p. 96.
(17) *Ibid.*, p. 95 (the quotation is from *Democracy in America*, vol. 1, chap. 12).

(1958) and in "On Violence." Such citizen-based, horizontal power can be used by the oppressed to rectify injustices perpetuated by their government and humanize their society.

The problem of conscience

The other important topic that Arendt addresses in "Civil Disobedience" is the problem of conscience. She views this topic through the lens of Western philosophy and history, beginning with the trial and death of Socrates. Although she did not develop her critique of conscience in great detail, her discussion reflects brilliant insights and illuminates aspects of the problem usually unnoticed even in more elaborate treatments of the subject. Socrates had the opportunity to escape death by fleeing Athens with the help of his friend Crito. But Socrates declared that if he disregarded the laws of Athens and became a fugitive, he would not be able to live *kalos* — a Greek term with a range of meanings including "beautiful," "good," and "well." If he decided to escape from his homeland, he would not be able to live a noble, good, or beautiful life. Here, he did not have creature comforts in mind. Rather, for Socrates living well required, first and foremost, living in harmony with one's true self — with his inner *daimon* (*daimonion*), as he says in *The Apology*. The moral import of this conviction appears in Socrates' statement in the *Gorgias*, where against the moral nihilism of Callicles he says that "it is better to suffer wrong than to do wrong" — a phrase that Arendt repeatedly cites as the essence of following one's conscience.[18] For Socrates, she says, it was of ultimate importance to live in accord with himself. Thus, being wronged at the hands of evil men was better for him than doing evil, just as it was better "to be in disagreement with the multitude rather than, being one [with the multitude], to be in disagreement with [oneself]."[19]

Historically, within Christianity, to live in accord with oneself acquired the meaning of living in harmony with one's conscience, understood as the

(18) *Ibid.*, p. 62 (the quotation is from *Gorgias*, 469a–491c).
(19) *Ibid.*, p. 62 (the quotation is from Gorgias, 482c).

inner voice of God. Conscience has become an inner court within human beings that, when summoned in emergencies, can direct humans to take the right action. This inner voice is often understood in religious terms, but it can also be based on personal, non-religious convictions. In either case, it functions as a regulative principle to control human actions and behaviors. Albert Camus, who was not a religious man in the conventional sense, nevertheless, taught that when an individual resists injustice he does so for the individual's "*own health and welfare.*" (20) He was obviously addressing the individual's moral health and welfare, which may not coincide with one's physical or financial well-being.

3. Developing Arendt's Views — The Dynamics of Civil Disobedience

Although Arendt's contribution to the literature on civil disobedience is limited, her ideas offer great potential for further development within the context of a broader political theory. The following discussion goes beyond Arendt's arguments to present my own ideas, inspired and informed by the basic framework contained in Arendt's theoretical reflections.

The dynamics of civil disobedience

As shown in Figure 1, movements of civil disobedience apparently have a threefold structure. First, there is (1) a *core group* of activists who initiate the movement by refusing to obey what they view as an unjust or immoral law or policy. Each member of the core group has made an individual decision to disobey the law, and to do so publicly. These are the actual disobedients. Second, are (2) those who do not break the law themselves but are *participants in protest actions*, such as boycotts or public demonstrations,

(20) *Ibid.*, p. 64 (the quotation is from Christian Bay, "Civil Disobedience," in the *International Encyclopedia of the Social Sciences*, 1968, vol. 2, p. 486; emphasis by Arendt).

Figure 1: Depiction of the spread of a movement of civil disobedience

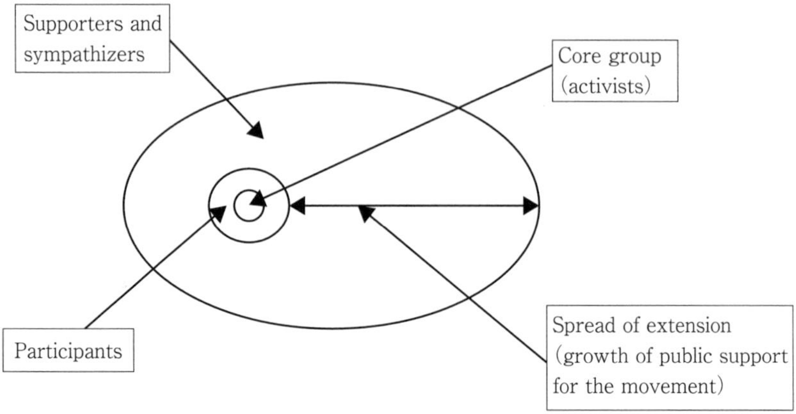

supporting the actual disobedients. These people form what Arendt (following Tocqueville) calls a "voluntary association." Finally, there is (3) a broader group of *supporters and sympathizers* who, while not engaging in either protest or disobedience actions, agree with the moral rightness of the protesters and disobedients. This larger group will often draw its strength from those of a similar ethnic, religious, gender, age, or socio-economic background as the disobedients and protesters, and they will also often be new converts to their supporting role, having previously been neutral or indifferent toward the aims of the core group and other protesters.

Since political power, as Arendt teaches, is often dependent on numbers, [21] the core group in successful civil disobedience campaigns must attract large numbers of participants and supporters through its symbolic acts in defiance of unjust laws. It is important, however, that this defiance be nonviolent, for the use of violence causes the civil disobedience campaign to lose the moral high ground and much of its broader appeal. The general public feels sympathy for those who refrain from injuring others in their

(21) See Hannah Arendt, "On Violence," in *Crises of the Republic*, New York: Harcourt Brace Jovanovich, 1972, pp. 140–141.

acts of civil disobedience, but this sympathy erodes if violence erupts. Successful civil disobedience movements, such as the one used by Martin Luther King, Jr. to protest segregation laws in the American South, succeed against established power by creating countervailing citizen power based on nonviolent persuasion and by changing the convictions of a large segment of the citizenry.

The political meaning of conscience

For both Thoreau and Arendt, the requirements of conscience are clearly limited. Thoreau stated that one should break the law only if the law is "of such a nature that it requires you to be the agent of injustice to another." (22) Unwise laws, foolish laws, and laws that arbitrarily favor one group over another should be changed, but they do not justify breaking the law. In contrast, laws that involve grave injustices are another matter and require civil disobedience.

Arendt states that when such grave injustices occur, "good men" often appear suddenly, "as if from nowhere, in all social strata." (23) She cites as an example Colonel George Picquart, a member of the French General Staff during the Dreyfus affair, who, despite the popularity of Dreyfus's conviction, concluded that the Jewish military officer was really innocent and that the evidence against him was fraudulent. For stating this opinion, the colonel paid a high price. "Picquart was banished to a dangerous post in Tunis," Arendt writes, and "he was [subsequently] drummed out of the army and divested of his decorations, all of which he endured with quiet equanimity." (24) Picquart, she continues, "was simply that common type of citizen with an average interest in public affairs who in the hour of danger stands up to

---

(22) "Civil Disobedience," p. 60; the quotation is from Henry D. Thoreau, "Resistance to Civil Government," in *Reform Papers*, ed. by Wendell Glick, Princeton: Princeton University Press, 1973 [1849], p. 73.

(23) *Ibid.*, p. 65.

(24) Hannah Arendt, *The Origins of Totalitarianism*, 3rd edition, New York: Harcourt, Brace & World, 1966, p. 109 (quoted from the footnote).

defend his country in the same unquestioning way as he discharges his daily duties."[25] Such a good man, Arendt believed, can save a whole people from descending into moral or political catastrophe.

In contrast to a savior figure like Picquart, Arendt describes Adolf Eichmann, the high-level Nazi official who organized the roundup of millions of European Jews and their transport to Nazi death camps. Learning from news reports that Eichmann had been arrested in Argentina in 1960 by the Israeli secret service, Arendt rearranged her 1961 schedule and offered herself as "a trial reporter" to *The New Yorker* magazine.[26] She filed journalistic reports on the Eichmann trial, and her reporting would later be published as a best-selling book, *Eichmann in Jerusalem: A Report on the Banality of Evil.* Arendt eagerly accepted the *New Yorker* assignment because she had not been present at the Nuremberg war crimes trial and she knew that this would probably be her last chance to observe a Nazi war criminal directly. She wanted to know, above all, what could drive someone like Eichmann to participate in the mass murder of millions of innocent people.

What she witnessed at Eichmann's trial was both surprising and deeply disturbing. Eichmann, she found, was not a hate-filled monster who relished the idea of rounding up Jews and sending them to gas chambers. In fact, he was not a Jew-hater at all, and he had a number of private reasons for not hating Jews: he had Jewish relatives on his mother's side and had a Jewish mistress when he lived in Vienna.[27] The only reason why he engaged in the mass murder of Jews was that he was a dutiful functionary in the Nazi bureaucracy and believed his first obligation was to obey lawful orders from his superiors — which, in the Nazi state, meant ultimately obeying the will

(25) *Ibid.*, p. 109.
(26) See Elisabeth Young-Bruehl, *Hannah Arendt: For Love of the World*, New Haven and London: Yale University Press, 1982, p. 328.
(27) See Hannah Arendt, *Eichmann in Jerusalem: A Report on the Banality of Evil*, New York: Viking Press, 1963, pp. 26–30.

of Adolf Hitler. As Hitler's orders had the power of law, Eichmann was functioning as simply a law-abiding citizen in carrying out the Holocaust. Eichmann was a very normal man within the context of this totalitarian state. He was "no exception within the Nazi regime," Arendt wrote. "Half a dozen psychiatrists had certified him as 'normal.'" [(28)]

At his trial Eichmann seemed to utter little more than banality and clichés, and Arendt concluded from this tendency that he lacked any capacity to think independently for himself. In a sense, he had no conscience or internal moral compass — or, rather, his conscience demanded that he obey the laws of the state regardless of their nature. "As for his conscience," Arendt wrote, "he remembered perfectly well that he would have had a bad conscience only if he had not done what he had been ordered to do — to ship millions of men, women, and children to their death with great zeal and the most meticulous care." [(29)] He was an utterly empty, bureaucratic careerist who mindlessly obeyed what the law required him to do. The reason why he felt no crisis of conscience, Arendt wrote, was that he lacked the ability of independent thought: "The longer one listened to him, the more obvious it became that his inability to speak was closely connected with an inability to *think*." [(30)]

In the same year as the appearance of *Eichmann in Jerusalem* (1963), Arendt published *On Revolution*, one of her most important works of political theory. In this work, which focuses on the world created by participants in modern revolutions, she addresses the ancient topic of the "hidden crime" — that is, "a criminal act witnessed by nobody and remaining unknown to all but its agent." [(31)] This question was also considered by both Socrates and Machiavelli. For the latter, a "hidden crime" is always known by God, so it always remains a crime. Arendt appreciates Socrates' perspective

(28) *Ibid.*, pp. 25–26.
(29) *Ibid.*, p. 25.
(30) *Ibid.*, p. 49 (emphasis by Arendt).
(31) Hannah Arendt, *On Revolution*, New York: Viking Press, 1963, p. 97.

Figure 2: Image of the "two-in-one" nature of human consciousness

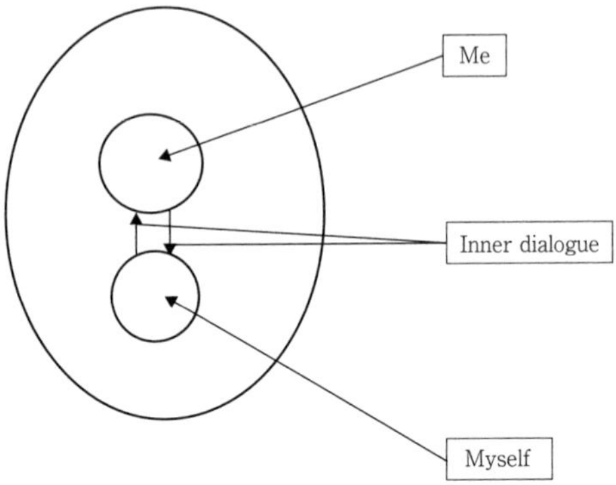

further: "Socrates' solution to the problem of the hidden crime was that there is nothing done by men which can remain 'unknown to men and gods.'" According to Socrates, one always carries within oneself a witness to what one does and which one cannot escape. Later ages, says Arendt, called this inner witness "conscience." (32) This involves a "two-in-one" (33) sense of human consciousness, a dialogue between "me and myself" that is an ongoing process of thought and reflection (see Figure 2).

In morally and intellectually healthy people, Arendt believed, this ongoing process of thought and reflection is a continuous, lifelong activity. Thinking in this sense becomes a major theme of Arendt's posthumously published *The Life of the Mind* (1978), edited by her close friend Mary McCarthy. In this work Arendt links the process of thinking, as she describes it, not simply with logical operations and means-ends rationality but with the human ability to distinguish right from wrong. She sees this ability as an indispensable faculty for being alive, enabling humans to live in a manner consistent with their convictions and to abstain from doing evil.

(32) *Ibid.*, p. 98.

(33) The term "two-in-one" first appeared in Arendt's book *On Revolution* (1963) but was more fully considered in her later work *The Life of the Mind*, vol. 1: *Thinking*, New York and London: Harcourt, Brace & Jovanovich, 1978, pp. 179–193.

Here again, Socrates is one of her role models. He represents for Arendt the quintessence of the morally and intellectually alive, thinking human being. "The meaning of what Socrates was doing," she writes, "lay in the activity [of thinking] itself. Or to put it differently: To think and to be fully alive are the same." (34) Thinking, in the pregnant sense in which Arendt uses the term, is closely tied to language and to such concepts as justice, happiness, and virtue. It is precisely the human activity in which a mindless bureaucrat like Eichmann is unable or unwilling to engage. The two-in-one, soundless dialogue of thinking that one has with oneself is the basis of conscience, and it demands above all that one not contradict oneself — in other words, that one remains true, as Socrates did, to one's inner voice. This inner dialogue often provides the basis for acting righteously, since acting in contradiction to one's higher beliefs and values creates a divided and discordant self, one that senses that something is profoundly wrong.

In addition to her analysis of thinking, Arendt spends considerable effort in analyzing the concepts of willing and promising. She sees human beings as centers of willful activity directed toward a future that is always uncertain. She categorically rejects any notion of psychological, volitional, or historical determinism. Thinking, acting people direct themselves toward a future that, unlike the past, is within their power to influence though not to control fully. To reduce the element of uncertainty and unpredictability about the future, and to enhance the possibility of creating a better future, it is necessary, Arendt believes, for thinking people to make promises and commitments, and then to stick to them as time passes. This is how the future is molded to conform more closely to the human will. In this context she presents her own rewriting of a statement by Thoreau. Thoreau had written: "The only obligation which I have a right to assume is to do at any time what I think right." (35) Arendt adds an emphasis on the importance of making and keeping promises and commitments that strive for a better future: "The only

(34) *Ibid.*, p. 178.
(35) "Resistance to Civil Government," p. 65.

obligation which I *as a citizen* have a right to assume is to make and to keep promises." (36)

Furthermore, Arendt has significant inputs on conscientious objection — the refusal on moral grounds to participate in a given war. John Rawls understood conscientious objection as a private act distinct from civil disobedience, which by definition is public and which, unlike conscientious objection, is primarily focused on changing public policy. Drawing on the experience of the American anti-war movement during the time of the Vietnam engagement, Arendt observes a closer connection than Rawls between conscientious objection and civil disobedience. If enough young men refuse, for reasons of conscience, to participate in a war — especially if they refuse because they believe that a given war is unjust or immoral — then their motivation and aims become identical to those of an organized movement of civil disobedience. Conscientious objection on a large scale, thus, has clear political implications and can change the power relationships in a democratic society. "Conscientious objection can become politically significant," Arendt writes, "when a number of conscientious objectors happen to coincide [with one another], and the conscientious objectors decide to enter the market place and make their voices heard in public." (37) Thus, the inner voices of individual war resisters can have significant political potential, and when combined with civil disobedience campaigns they can gain considerable public support.

It follows that, for Arendt, the inner world of conscience and one's own better self can play a crucial role in politics, and that it is especially important in time of moral and political crises when injustice threatens to gain the upper hand. It is important for any civic culture to cultivate the capacity for such self-reflection and examination of conscience, Arendt believes, and when these crucial capacities are cultivated, their positive effects can spill over to correct injustices caused by powerful business groups, administrative

(36) "Civil Disobedience," p. 92 (emphasis by Arendt).
(37) *Ibid.*, pp. 67–68.

organizations, and all other forms of organized power. Arendt's analysis requires that we think seriously about the best ways to cultivate the kind of conscience-driven moral reflection that will enable ordinary citizens to play a key role in making the world more just and humane. Both civil disobedience and conscientious objection are means of enhancing citizen power, and they can provide important checks on the tendency of large organizations, both governmental and non-governmental, to become oppressive and destructive of the public good.

4. Conclusion

A general tendency to obey the law is a necessary prerequisite for a decent and stable society. Knowing that laws will be generally obeyed brings comfort, stability, predictability, and security to any society. Lawlessness and general disrespect for law make any kind of higher civilization impossible; as Thomas Hobbes stated so forcefully, lawlessness renders human life "solitary, poor, nasty, brutish, and short." [38] But laws are sometimes unjust and oppressive, and even when democratically enacted they may embody evil and wicked intentions. Civil disobedience is an important means by which citizens can challenge unjust laws without recourse to violence or to civil war. It requires of those who engage in it a process of inner reflection and mature examination of conscience, together with an attempt to persuade others of the moral rightness of one's cause. Moral persuasion rather than violence is the source of its power — a power of which ordinary citizens can always avail themselves in concert with others.

Although Hannah Arendt is not regarded as a major theorist of civil disobedience, her overall philosophy provides a valuable framework for understanding the mechanisms of civil disobedience and how it operates to enhance citizen power through the vehicle of conscience and the inner

(38) See Thomas Hobbes, *Leviathan*, edited with an introduction by J. C. A. Gaskin, Oxford: Oxford University Press, 1996 [1651], p. 84.

dialogue that thinking human beings conduct with themselves. Socrates' attunement to the inner voice of his *daimon* is, for Arendt and others, the paradigmatic case of the kind of activity that all morally and spiritually alive human beings must undertake, particularly in times of grave moral crisis and political danger. Conversely, Adolf Eichmann represented for Arendt the paradigmatic case of the unthinking, cliché-ridden automaton, bereft of an active inner life or a voice of conscience. He was the anti-Socrates, and his lack of an inner moral compass led him to participate mindlessly in horrendous acts of cruelty and mass murder.

In movements of civil disobedience, the voice of conscience seeks like-minded people as allies to mobilize for citizen participation in politics. The aim is always to correct evils, whatever source they come from. Justice must always be the goal. Martin Luther King, Jr.'s civil rights movement in America and Mohandas K. Gandhi's earlier independence movement in India are models for the use of nonviolent civil disobedience to effect political change. They stand among the noblest exemplars in the 20th century of how citizen power and the power of mobilized righteousness can bring about greater justice and desirable social change. We can continue to turn to them for inspiration and guidance. Civil disobedience must always remain a legitimate alternative for citizens, and our civic culture must continue to encourage the kind of independent moral judgment and recourse to conscience that are a necessary prerequisite for the maintenance of any just society.

V

People Power and Nonviolent Revolution:
Hannah Arendt's Influence on Theories of Nonviolence

1. Introduction

Democratization is one aspect of globalization. In contrast to globalization in the areas of economy and culture, democratization movements come from below, from ordinary citizens. It is remarkable that in the years 2010-11, even in Middle Eastern countries, peoples could remove nondemocratic regimes through revolutions with nearly no violence.

Although, without further analysis, we cannot easily explain why a nonviolent way of changing political systems was taken, it is certain that Gene Sharp's theory of nonviolence had a great influence on this democratization movement. His theory of nonviolence is actualized based on what is called *strategic nonviolence*, which puts forward nonviolence from the viewpoint of strategy: nonviolent struggles are more effective and more likely to win against unjust systems or invasions by foreign troops, with fewer casualties, than violent ones. This concept stands in contrast to the concept of *principled nonviolence* — the position that nonviolence should be chosen as the correct path because it is ethically right. However, one should bear in mind that strategic nonviolence is not the opposite concept of principled nonviolence. Although he started his academic career as a student of nonviolence from the study of Mohandas Gandhi as a political strategist[(1)] and he is presently called "the Clausewitz of nonviolent warfare," [(2)] Gene Sharp was a conscientious objector at the time of the Korean War and was jailed for more than 9 months for taking this stand. He also seems to be a pacifist, but he has not disclosed his own beliefs. It is important that people taking the position of strategic nonviolence emphasize the effectiveness of nonviolence and in fact improve the techniques and skills of nonviolent struggle.

The most important point in the development of this study is that Sharp's theory of nonviolence focuses on a theoretical analysis of power. If we learned the sources of power, he argues, we could remove a dictatorship by attacking the weaknesses of its regime. As Max Weber recognized, no government could sustain itself without the support and cooperation of its subjected population. Therefore, if the people do not give their support to the government, even a dictatorship is likely to collapse. The power of nonviolent movements is different from political power in the ordinary use of the term. It is the power of a united people that needs to be understood as "horizontal," although power is usually understood as being "vertical" and connected with violence. Hannah Arendt changed this concept of power into a new concept of power, which is outlined in her major work *The Human Condition* (1958) and her article on violence (1969), the latter of which was originally published under the title "Reflections on Violence" [(3)] and later expanded and reprinted as "On Violence" in her book *Crises of the Republic* (1972).

As we later see, Arendt's political theory, particularly her concept of power, influenced theorists of nonviolence such as Gene Sharp and Michael

---

(1) Gene Sharp, *Gandhi as a Political Strategist: with Essays on Ethics and Politics*, Boston: Porter Sargent Publishers, 1979.

(2) Roger S. Powers, "Sharp, Gene," in *Protest, Power, and Change: An Encyclopedia of Nonviolent Action from ACT-UP to Women's Suffrage*, editors, Roger S. Powers, William B. Vogele; associate editors, Christopher Kruegler, Ronald M. McCarthy, New York and London: Garland, 1997, p. 467.

(3) Hannah Arendt, "Reflections on Violence," *Journal of International Affairs*, vol. 23, no. 1 (Winter 1969), pp. 1–35.

Randle. It is said that her book *On Revolution* (1963) had "a delayed effect" (4) on revolutionary movements in Eastern European countries after the 1980s, similar to its impact on the formation of participatory democracy theory in the 1960s, the "renaissance of civil society," and the rise of new republicanism. (5)

The potential power of her political theory lies in making politics more humane; in particular, her concept of power contributes to the influence of nonviolent political change, which can be used to change the world and achieve humane values without violence. The purpose of this article is to show comprehensively the linkage between Arendt's concept of power and the theory of nonviolence developed by Sharp.

2. Hannah Arendt's Theory of Power

The concept of power in *The Origins of Totalitarianism*

In her first major political book, *The Origins of Totalitarianism* (1951), Arendt analyzed totalitarianism as a political phenomenon and depicted all negative aspects of politics at full length. According to Arendt, under totalitarian regimes power should be understood as being exercised vertically, transmitting commands from above to below. She argues that one important feature of totalitarianism is the leader principle (the English translation for the German word *Führerprinzip*), while the other features are terror and ideology. In the leader principle, the source of power is vested in

(4) Elisabeth Young-Bruehl, one of her students at the New School for Social Research in New York, wrote a detailed biography of Hannah Arendt, in which she remarked that "*On Revolution* did have a delayed effect" (*Hannah Arendt: For Love of the World*, New Haven and London: Yale University Press, 1982, p. 404). The book was widely read by students interested in political theory in the 1960s and by people concerned with nonviolent civil resistance in the 1980s.

(5) The new type of republicanism has nothing to do with the patriotism and public virtues in the old type of republicanism exemplified by the political thoughts of Machiavelli and Rousseau.

the will of the leader, that is to say, the dictator. The subjects who surround the leader can do nothing but whatever is ordered by him. Thus, the concept of power is the same as that in its usual usage, or even more vertical than an ordinary power relationship.

It must be remarked that in this book the concept of power remains as usually used, even as she harshly criticizes totalitarian power. A characteristic of the leader principle is rule by one man's will. It dates from the characteristics of earlier totalitarian movements, which formed hierarchically around the leadership. The leader has absolute power over his subjects, as Arendt writes, so he "cannot tolerate criticism of his subordinates, since they act always in his name; if he wants to correct his own errors, he must liquidate those who carried them out; if he wants to blame his mistakes on others, he must kill them." (6) She characterizes this situation as total responsibility. But it should be noted that she recognizes that a leader's power depends on the support and assistance of the people, in the same way that "the commander's power is dependent on the whole hierarchic system in which he operates." (7) In relation to this hierarchical structure, although power is grasped as order and obedience, it is important that she recognizes that power depends on the people's support. Ideology and terror are employed to strengthen the basis of the leader's power: ideology serves to lead the people into believing in the future society toward which the regime aims; terror is employed to destroy the plurality of human beings and to make "out of many the One who unfailingly will act as though he himself were part of the course of history and nature" (8) by frightening the people who inherently differ from person to person. The authority of the regime is monopolized by the leader. Generally speaking, gigantic organizations are authority-oriented and thus able to strengthen their own

---

(6) Hannah Arendt, *The Origins of Totalitarianism*, 3rd edition, New York: Harcourt, Brace & World, Inc., 1966, p. 375.

(7) *Ibid.*, p. 364.

(8) *Ibid.*, p. 466.

power. Totalitarian power is a type of rule by a dictator, but Arendt points out that even such a power depends on the endorsement of the subjects.

While the concept of power in *The Origins of Totalitarianism* focuses on the relationship between the leader and the people, where does the horizontal concept of power, which she develops in her later works, come from? It is important to bear in mind that she believes totalitarian power destroys politics. The prototype of Arendt's political theory can be seen in this book, and its most important conclusion is the recognition that politics is based on human plurality. Totalitarian power is contrary to plurality in that it is set in motion by one man's will. It is based on singularity in several aspects, such as its intention to change many people into one people and its domination by the dictator's will. Arendt argues that totalitarian terror "substitutes for the boundaries channels of communication between individual men a band of iron which holds them so tightly together that it is as though their plurality had disappeared into One Man of gigantic dimensions." [(9)] In the political theory of Arendt there is almost no place for sovereignty, because it rests on the will of the one, whether the will of the dictator or that of the people. In contrast, power is related to plurality and, therefore, linked to politics in her political theory. As plurality is a condition of action, it seems to her, power must be redefined as the basic condition for republican politics, which cherishes citizens' voluntary participation.

Where does Arendt's concept of power come from?

The change in Arendt's concept of power first comes from her reading the political works of Montesquieu and Tocqueville in the early 1950s. She learned much from their thoughts that power could be checked by power and that freedom is closely connected with power. Her concept of power was greatly influenced by Montesquieu. In February 1952, she wrote on the division of power in *Denktagebuch*: "The essential point is the need to

(9) *Ibid*., pp. 465–466.

recognize that power is not only controllable — this was well known by Romans — but also divisible, without which loss of power thereby happens, or the quality of power disappears. This means that sovereignty is not the primary definition of power. Power is not a phenomenon of will, and neither made by wills, nor primarily the object of wills." (10)

Second, the change comes from Arendt's encounter with American political thought and culture. From the late 1940s, she continually read works by the Founding Fathers of the Republic of the USA. Before she obtained US citizenship in 1951, Arendt learned a bit about American history, as she wrote, "For my citizenship test, for rather in celebration of it, I have learnt a little American constitutional history." (11) In the 1950s she began full-fledged study of the history of the American Revolution. She conveyed her ideas in "On the Concept of Revolution," a lecture she gave at Princeton University in 1958, which formed the foundation of her book entitled *On Revolution* (1963). During this period, she passionately read the works of the Founding Fathers, in particular *The Federalist Papers*, and discovered many basic principles in relation to politics, one of which is the enlargement of power in the history of the American Revolution. In the political constitution and institutions of the United States, there are many signs of power that can be horizontally constituted in the process of the revolution.

In *On Revolution* she characterizes revolution as "the foundation of freedom," but she had grasped the real positive meaning of freedom much earlier. After she landed in New York, she immediately encountered a free atmosphere and was moved by a culture where freedom was not merely an idea but reality. It is an important aspect of her political theory to connect freedom with power. She understood freedom in a positive sense

(10) Hannah Arendt, *Denktagebuch, 1950 bis 1973*, hrsg. von Ursula Ludz und Ingeborg Nordmann, in Zusammenarbeit mit dem Hannah-Arendt-Institut, Dresden: Piper, 2002, p. 184 (underlined by Arendt).

(11) Hannah Arendt to Karl Jaspers, September 28, 1951, in Hannah Arendt/Karl Jaspers, *Hannah Arendt/Karl Jaspers Briefwechsel 1926–1969*, hrsg. von Lotte Köhler und Hans Saner, München: Piper, 1985, p. 209.

in contrast to the concept of liberty: In her book, the former means active participation in government, while the latter means the result of liberation from oppression. Since acting actively generates power, it is the essential prerequisite for freedom.

Third, and most importantly, the change in her view of power comes from her discovery of the concept of plurality, which dates back to the late 1940s, when she thought about the mechanism of totalitarianism. She saw the fundamentals for politics in what totalitarianism denied. One of them is plurality, which is, according to her, the most basic condition for human existence, and which she calls the human condition itself. To be a human being requires certain conditions. We must be aware that human beings are by definition plural and at the same time have features of equality and distinction, in other words, commonness and uniqueness. Each human being is distinguished from anyone who is, was, or will ever be; (12) that is, there is nobody who is quite the same as anyone else in the past, present, or future.

In the 1950s, Arendt tried to establish a new science of politics, as she quotes Tocqueville's words, "A new science of politics is needed for a new world." (13) Although her project was not completed, parts of her thinking were shaped in her works from the 1950s to 1970s. The major works are *The Human Condition* and *On Revolution*, but also in "On Violence" her fundamental political concepts are clarified. The intent is to place politics in ordinary human life by recovering the authentic meaning of the political experiences of those who have spontaneously taken part in politics, from ancient Greece to modern revolutions. In this context, politics is the interaction among people who are distinct from each other. While sovereignty is connected to singularity, or one man's will, power is connected to human plurality, which constitutes the potentiality of action. Therefore,

(12) See Hannah Arendt, *The Human Condition*, Chicago: The University of Chicago Press, 1958, p. 175.

(13) *Denktagebuch, 1950 bis 1973*, Heft XIX (Januar 1954), p. 465 (this passage is quoted from the preface to *Democracy in America*, vol. 1, by Tocqueville in 1835).

power must be redefined in order to build the framework of a new science of politics.

Power and action

According to Arendt, action is closely connected with speech. Aristotle defined man as *zōon politikon* (political animal), but this definition becomes meaningful only by his second definition of human beings as "*zōon logon ekhon*" (a living being capable of speech). When men act, speech is always accompanied with action. The condition for action is for human beings to live together, which means not just being together but living in confidence and cooperation. Living-togetherness is a potential condition for generating action. When a man initiates something new, he finds fellow people with whom to conduct the action. On this point, the concept of action is connected with that of power. As she writes, "The only indispensable material factor in the generation of power is the living together of people. Only where men live so close together that the potentialities of action are always present can power remain with them, and the foundation of cities, which as city-states are paradigmatic for all Western political organizations, is the most important prerequisite for power."(14) In sum, men need to have a political realm such as a *polis* in order to continue action. But, Arendt continues, "the *polis*, properly speaking, is not the city-state in its physical location; it is the organization of the people as it arises out of acting and speaking together, and its true space lies between people living together for this purpose, no matter where they happen to be. 'Where you go, you will be a *polis*'; these famous words became not merely the watchword of Greek colonization, they expressed the conviction that action and speech create a space between the participants which can find its proper location almost any time and anywhere." (15)

It is Arendt's conviction that we can create power, and its condition is the living together of people. Power derives from the potentiality that can

(14) *The Human Condition*, p. 201.
(15) *Ibid.*, p. 198.

be generated by people who want to act in concert. She clarifies her notion as "power springs up between men when they act together and vanishes the moment they disperse." (16) While power is kept in the public realm, men can newly create power. "What keeps people together after the fleeting moment of action has passed (what we today call 'organization') and what, at the same time, they keep alive through remaining together is power." (17) The potential character of power is, according to Arendt, free from such epistemological facts as implied by *dynamis*, the Greek equivalent for power, the Latin *potentia* along with its modern derivatives, or the German word Macht (which derives from *mögen* and *möglich*). (18) In her work of political theory, *The Human Condition*, she points to the effectiveness of nonviolent struggle, since popular revolt "may engender an almost irresistible power even if it forgoes the use of violence in the face of materially vastly superior forces." (19)

As stated earlier, Arendt planned to construct a new science of politics, which would extensively examine fundamental political concepts. She wished to free politics from domination and to position it at the level of ordinary people's lives. Fundamental political concepts must be redefined from this perspective. She tried to find out hidden meanings in political concepts. Language is the treasury of the experiences of humankind. By thinking in this way, she developed horizontal political concepts. Although her project on the principles of politics, whose manuscript was entitled "Introduction into Politics," had not been completed, her reflections on political fundamentals remained a constant part of her writings. One of them is her essay "On Violence," reflections on the concept of violence, in which she contrasted violence with power.

Arendt engaged in distinguishing concepts and tried to clarify the

---

(16) *Ibid.*, p. 200.
(17) *Ibid.*, p. 201.
(18) *Ibid.*, p. 200.
(19) *Ibid.*, pp. 200–201.

differences among similar concepts. It is important for her to separate power from violence. In order to do so, she had to criticize the traditional concept of power, which had equated power with violence. Of course, this is implicit in her analysis of totalitarianism as a phenomenon where power involves violence in politics. The ultimate power of the state is the power of life and death on subjects. It becomes possible for the state to monopolize violent means. But conceptually, power can be clearly distinguished from violence. According to Arendt, while violence depends on instruments, and works in extreme cases, One against All, as shown in the case of a pistol gang that threatens people with a gun to gain their obedience, power depends on the number of people who support it, and "the extreme form of power is All against One." (20) "*Power* corresponds to the human ability not just to act but to act in concert. Power is never the property of an individual; it belongs to a group and remains in existence only if the group keeps together." (21) The difference lies in the fact that violence rests on weapons, but "the power of the government rests on numbers; it is "in proportion to 'the number with which it is associated.'" (22)

Then, how can we link power with nonviolence? As stated above, Arendt separated power from violence and linked it to the number of its adherents. According to her, "it is not correct to think of the opposite of violence as nonviolence; to speak of nonviolent power is actually redundant." (23) That is to say, power inherently has a nonviolent character, so it is superfluous to add nonviolence to the concept of power. Moreover, in fact Arendt thinks of power as the opposite of violence and recognizes that power can be more effectively generated by nonviolent movements. When she wrote this article, there were nonviolent resistance activities in Czechoslovakia

(20) Hannah Arendt, "On Violence," in *Crises of the Republic*, New York: Harcourt Brace Jovanovich, 1972, p. 141.
(21) *Ibid.*, p. 143 (emphasis by Arendt).
(22) *Ibid.*, p. 140 (quoted from *The Federalist*, No. 49).
(23) *Ibid.*, p. 155.

and anti-Vietnam War movements in the United States, and these events inspired her to think about the fundamentals of politics. On the one hand, she wrote "Violence can always destroy power; out of the barrel of a gun grows the most effective command, resulting in the most instant and perfect obedience," (24) but on the other hand, she emphasized the historical fact that nonviolent resistance can liberate oppressed people and establish freedom, as illustrated in the case of the Gandhi-led movements in India. It is said that in 1967 she admitted that nonviolence was essential not only for tactical reasons but also for "the enormous power of nonviolence." (25) She considered many cases of nonviolent resistance in contemporary history and characterized the case of nonviolent resistance in Czechoslovakia as "a textbook case of a confrontation between violence and power in their pure states." (26) In a well-known passage from "On Violence," she stated, "If Gandhi's enormously powerful and successful strategy of nonviolent resistance had met with a different enemy — Stalin's Russia, Hitler's Germany, even prewar Japan, instead of England — the outcome would not have been decolonization, but massacre and submission." (27) But, it must be noted, the focus lies in the observation that although violence can bring victory, the price is high, since it certainly undermines the bases of power.

Power and violence usually appear together, but it is necessary to distinguish the essential features of these two concepts. When power is lost among people and a feeling of impotence spreads through them, sheer violence is able to rule them, as historical facts show. Since it is not possible to banish the love for freedom from people's minds, there always remains the possibility of resistance, and her theory of power shows that power is based on the consent of people and therefore can be generated at anytime, wherever people live in cooperation and confidence. Power is also dependent

---

(24) *Ibid.*, p. 152.
(25) *Hannah Arendt: For Love of the World*, p. 414.
(26) "On Violence," in *Crises of the Republic*, p. 152.
(27) *Ibid.*, p. 152.

on a nonviolent way of life, and it makes power more powerful when people act in concert without employing violent means.

3. Nonviolent Struggle and People Power

The Gandhian moment

It was Mohandas Gandhi, who most prominently made nonviolence an effective way of struggle against oppression. He was very much influenced by the ideas of Henry David Thoreau on the practice of civil disobedience, but in contrast to Thoreau, Gandhi was an organizer and activist. He developed civil resistance as a collective action and led many movements in South Africa and India.

As Michael Randle, one of the most important theorists on nonviolent civil resistance, writes in his major book, *Civil Resistance* (1994), "the figure whose actions and ideas have crucially influenced the development of civil resistance in the twentieth century is Mohandas K. Gandhi — 'Mahatma' Gandhi." [28] Gandhi is important in that he combined the ethics of nonviolence with political movements and established the discipline of nonviolence within such movements. Although nonviolent resistance evolved in the 19th century and earlier collective actions for democratization were chiefly done nonviolently, Gandhi is the first who consciously employed nonviolence, organizing mass civil disobedience movements. In the nonviolent resistance in South Africa, he decided to change "passive resistance" into "*satyagraha*" in order to express a positive meaning of the movement he intended to found. He learned much from the past struggles waged nonviolently in Europe, but he himself had much more influence on nonviolent movements all over the world. Thus, we can say that his movements have special significance for students of nonviolence.

Gene Sharp, one of the leading advocates of nonviolent struggle, is

---

(28) Michael Randle, *Civil Resistance*, London: Fontana Press, 1994, p. 52.

among those who were strongly influenced by Gandhi. He started his study of nonviolence by characterizing Gandhi as a political strategist. He adopted the words of Krishnalal Shridharani, who observed Gandhi's struggle and described it as "war without violence." (29) Although he was morally attached to nonviolence, Gandhi was also a strategist and deliberately used nonviolent techniques of struggle for national liberation struggles. According to Sharp, the following point is important: "Nonviolent action became not passive resistance but a technique capable of taking the initiative in active struggle." (30)

Gandhi devised various means to remove oppression from the colonial government. He testified that nonviolence would work well in collective civil resistance. It is important that he obtained insight into the nature of power. Sharp argues that Gandhi saw voluntary servitude as a basis of governmental power, further commenting, "Gandhi saw this view of the basis of the regime's power as fully compatible with the recognition of the importance of wielding power of some type in order to change relationships between the rulers and the ruled." (31) The point is to change the power relationship between the two parties. In order to achieve such a change, we need to have more power than the oppressor. Nonviolent means are never used to injure others. Rather, nonviolent resisters themselves would suffer instead. By exerting this moral superiority, the resisters can get more support and sympathy among previously indifferent people. This is how nonviolent struggle can gain more and more power and lead to victory over the rulers, provided the resisters persistently struggle with oppression by nonviolent means.

---

(29) Sharp mentions the words "war without violence" in his book on Gandhi (*Gandhi as a Political Strategist: with Essays on Ethics and Politics*, pp. 315–318). This is also the title of Krishnalal Shridharani's study of Gandhi (*War without Violence: A Study of Gandhi's Method and Its Accomplishments*, New York: Harcourt Brace, and Co., 1939).

(30) *Gandhi as a Political Strategist: with Essays on Ethics and Politics*, p. 14.

(31) *Ibid.*, p. 49.

As Randle observed, Gandhi is the figure who developed the way of struggle from passive resistance to *satyagraha*. Within the whole history of nonviolent struggle, Gandhi's importance lies in the establishment of nonviolent discipline and its testament to the effectiveness of nonviolent action. His thoughts and struggles were based on nonviolence, and his convictions on nonviolence advanced gradually, opening up new political dimensions. He shaped a paradigmatic historic example, which is followed by people who consciously engaged in removing violations of human rights and dictatorships. Gandhi's *satyagraha* was a positive way of struggle that led to people power, which was a term coined to express the power of a people united to bring about the nonviolent Philippine Revolution of 1986.

The birth of the concept of "power of nonviolence"

It was not Gene Sharp but Richard Gregg who created the term "power of nonviolence." Gregg observed Gandhi's struggle as one of his contemporaries and was very much moved. He interpreted Gandhi's type of struggle as an effective means of struggle and wanted to replace war with nonviolent resistance. Because "non-violent resistance is a safer and more effective instrument of policy," [32] it should replace war.

Between the two world wars, the most crucial fear was the threat of yet another war, and pacifist movements developed in Western countries. Gregg learned much from Gandhi and developed the argument to employ nonviolent resistance as a policy and, moreover, raised the possibility of nonviolent power defeating over military force. His argument is also based on the creation of power by nonviolence.

---

(32) Richard B. Gregg, *The Power of Nonviolence*, Philadelphia: J. B. Lippincott, 1934, p. 157.

4. From People Power to Nonviolent Revolution

Sharp's concept of power

Although Gandhi's theory of nonviolence has greatly influenced subsequent nonviolent struggles throughout the world, particularly in the United States and South Africa, Gandhi himself was also much influenced by the thoughts of Lev Tolstoy on nonviolence and of H. D. Thoreau on civil disobedience, as well as being affected by the previous nonviolent struggles of the 19th century in Europe. Therefore, it is difficult to clearly assess his influence on the historical events that followed. In a similar way, we have difficulties in estimating Arendt's influence on the theories of nonviolence. However, it is certain that her concept of power has provided a firm foundation for the development of the concept of power from state power to people power, which is based on the voluntary cooperation of ordinary citizens.

In particular, Sharp has admitted influences from Arendt, particularly regarding the horizontal concept of power. In *Exploring Nonviolent Alternatives*, he writes "True power, it seemed, came not from the barrels of [one's] guns, but from the power of a united people." (33) This characterization of power is an echo of Arendt's distinction between power and violence. It is certain that he was greatly influenced by her works on power, (34) *On Revolution* and "On Violence." Although she also argues about power in *The Human Condition*, he says he did not read the work at full length. It seems that he learned much from her distinction of power from violence and her notion that power can emerge from working together with other people.

(33) Gene Sharp, *Exploring Nonviolent Alternatives*, Boston: Porter Sargent Publishers, 1970, p. 21.

(34) I could ascertain that Sharp was much influenced by Arendt's theory of power when I talked with him at the Conference on "Civil Resistance and Power Politics" at Oxford University in March 2007.

"Acting together" or "acting in concert" is a source of power — this is the recognition that Sharp shares with Arendt.

Wars and violent conflicts are in contrast with nonviolent struggles not only in the difference between violent and nonviolent but also at a deeper level: While violent struggles demand a vertical relationship, secrecy and one-dimensionality among combatants, in nonviolent struggles an equal relationship among participants is important. This is because it is necessary for them to communicate their will to others and to cooperate through speech and action,[35] as Arendt insists in *The Human Condition*. Nonviolence is closely connected to this type of democracy, which is based on the initiatives of free individuals.

Why power is important in nonviolent struggles

In his first major work, *The Politics of Nonviolent Action* (1973), Sharp had already given attention to the concept of power, and the title of the first part of his book is "Power and Struggle." His concept of power dates back from the social analysis of power, similar to how Max Weber analyzed the legitimacy of rule in his study on the sociology of rule in *Economy and Society*. While Weber's arguments on the legitimacy of rule are based on the support of the ruled, or the psychological aspects, Sharp's arguments focus on the sources of power because he recognized that power through the voluntary obedience of the ruled is strong enough to be stably maintained.

Sharp discerned the following six factors as sources of power in "Power and Struggle": (1) authority, "which is voluntarily accepted by the people and therefore existing without the imposition of sanctions," (2) human resources, which affect a ruler's power because they "cooperate with him, or provide him with special assistance," (3) skills and knowledge, which also affect a ruler's power, (4) intangible factors, which are "psychological and ideological factors, such as habits and attitudes toward obedience and submission, and

(35) See *The Human Condition*, p. 179.

the presence or absence of a common faith, ideology, or sense of mission," (5) material resources, which are "the degree to which the ruler controls property, natural resources, financial resources, the economic system, means of communication and transportation, which help to determine the limits of his power," and (6) sanctions, which are at the disposal of a ruler "both for use against his own subjects and in conflicts with other rulers." [(36)]

These arguments come from a stream of political thought beginning with Étienne de La Boétie (1530-63) on "voluntary servitude". Therefore, we should say that not only Arendt but also other thinkers on power have affected Sharp's understanding of political power. However, Arendt's influence on Sharp is crucial in the distinction between power and violence, and he develops her concept of power as a tool in theorizing nonviolent struggles. In the 1970s and 80s, Sharp's concerns were directed toward civilian-based defense, which was proposed as a policy to substitute military-based defense by non-military defense, not only by Sharp but also by Adam Roberts, Theodore Ebert and others. Civilian-based defense was a term coined by Sharp in order to clarify its difference from military defense and to stress that the agents of defense are ordinary people. They avoided using the term "nonviolent defense" because this had been used by pacifists and sounds like something related to religious beliefs. They would instead prefer to emphasize the *strategic effectiveness* of nonviolence as a defense policy. Although it may seem to be a utopian project, they insist on the feasibility of the idea. Among all of the advocates of civilian-based defense, Sharp has most consistently and fully developed the concept.

In the 1960s, the civil rights movement developed and acquired positive results. The movement was carried out by nonviolent means and testified to the effectiveness of nonviolent struggle. In Europe, there is a history of nonviolent resistance against Nazi occupation in Denmark, the Netherlands, and Norway. In general it is believed that even if nonviolent resistance

---

(36) See Gene Sharp, *The Politics of Nonviolent Action*, Part 1, Boston: Porter Sargent Publishers, 1973, pp. 11-12.

can be effective and succeed in cases of domestic conflict, it would not be so effective nor successful in cases of invasion and occupation by foreign troops. Consequently, the purpose of civilian-based defense is to promote the effectiveness of nonviolent action by describing as many examples as possible in which it defeated its opponents, thus highlighting the potential of nonviolence. This must be done by theorizing methods of nonviolent action. Previously, even domestic struggles were carried out violently. Therefore, it is a core point of nonviolence for Sharp to insist on substituting violent struggles with nonviolent ones.

At that time, in the Cold War years, there was the possibility of nuclear war, and if nuclear war had broken out, humankind would have been put at enormous risk. Advocates of civilian-based defense have suggested nonviolent civilian defense as an alternative policy from a pragmatic perspective. Pragmatic not only because it stresses effectiveness but also because it searches for commonsense conviction from humankind's collective experiences of nonviolent action. There are many cases of nonviolent struggles that produced creative results. Sharp explored concrete examples all over the world and, in 1973, completed a three-volume work on nonviolent action entitled *The Politics of Nonviolent Action.* (37)

His theory of civilian-based defense is an application of nonviolent struggles, which have as long a history as the history of war. According to Sharp, it "has nothing to do with the question of 'pacifism' as it has traditionally been posed." (38) Civilian-based defense has been advocated from the viewpoint of strategic nonviolence: If a people coped with military aggression through nonviolent methods such as boycotts and strikes, they could defeat the aggressors. However, even if this were the case, civilian-based defense has been considered unrealistic and unorthodox as a national defense policy, due to the strongly held idea of ordinary people that a nation

(37) *The Politics of Nonviolent Action,* Parts 1–3, Boston: Porter Sargent Publishers, 1973.

(38) *Exploring Nonviolent Alternatives,* p. 26.

cannot be defended without military force.

But it is also a fact that in the 20th century successful examples of nonviolent struggles have occurred throughout the world. Sharp argues, therefore, "It is, perhaps, not without significance that the emergence of this technique to prominence in the political arena has taken place in the same half-century as the emergence of the totalitarian State and nuclear war. On the one hand is power which relies on suppression and destruction. On the other, is power relying on noncooperation, intervention, and nonviolent moral courage." (39) It is important to note his contrasting uses of the word power. For he thinks that it is the power of ordinary people that could make civilian-based defense a realistic concept of defense.

Sharp is consistently concerned with the problem of power. But his notion of power is horizontal and nonviolent, which is due to Arendt's influence on his theory of nonviolent action. He takes further steps toward the advocacy of a defense policy. The key concept of his nonviolence theory is based on our recent tendency to substitute violent conflicts with nonviolent conflicts. This process has proceeded gradually. In fields such as labor disputes, minority group grievances, peasant struggles, and colonial liberation movements, methods have already been evolving from violence to nonviolence. Although in the area of national defense such a substitution has not yet occurred, if we wish to achieve a world without war, it is necessary to think about a realistic way to achieve the abolition of war. (40)

The spread of nonviolent revolution

Since the 1980s in the field of revolution, nonviolent revolution has become mainstream, as exemplified in the cases of the People Power Revolution in the Philippines in 1986 and the nonviolent revolutions in Eastern Europe in 1989. In both cases, Sharp engaged in the process as an

(39) *Ibid.*, p. 22.

(40) See Gene Sharp, *Making Abolition of War a Realistic Goal*, New York: World Policy Institute, 1980.

observer on the spot (in the Philippines) or a consultant (in independent nonviolent struggles in Baltic countries). Of particular note is that his books on civilian-based defense were translated into the Lithuanian and Latvian languages, and in fact nonviolent defense was put into practice in order to defend Lithuania's newly proclaimed independence against military intervention by Soviet special troops in 1989.

It is not a coincidence that Arendt's book on revolution was well read among people who participated in the 1989 revolutionary movements in Eastern Europe. Her book, *On Revolution*, has an emotional power over its readers due to its ability to describe modern and contemporary revolutions as vivid epics, a power totally lacking in Sharp's writings. The point understood by modern revolutionaries is that we can create power from below and change the world. In the last chapter of the book, Arendt tells a sad and forgotten story about the council system, which spontaneously appeared in the process of revolutions but was crushed by the power of the party system and bureaucracy, as a lost treasure. This is a type of radical democracy whose foundation is found in the people themselves. In her time, she witnessed the Hungarian Revolution of 1956, which aroused her interest to the point that she incorporated its developments in her books on totalitarianism [(41)] and revolution. She paid attention to the rapid formation of the council system in the Hungarian Revolution and to the fact that, under such repressive political regimes as the totalitarian systems, freedom-loving people were able to resist and launch a revolution.

Since the mid-1980s, Sharp's main concern gradually shifted from civilian-based defense to nonviolent revolution, in pace with actual events around the world. Although he did not lose interest in defense problems, Sharp responded to new phases of democratization in the contemporary world. Bringing down dictatorships had become a realistic matter and an urgent

---

(41) See Hannah Arendt, "Epilogue: Reflections on the Hungarian Revolution," in *The Origins of Totalitarianism*, Second enlarged edition, New York: World Publishing Co., Meridian Books, 1958, pp. 480–510.

agenda to deal with. *From Dictatorship to Democracy* was first published in Bangkok in 1993 (42) in order to offer "some guidelines to assist thought and planning to produce movements of liberation that are more powerful and effective than might otherwise be the case." (43)

It is a key point to attack the weaknesses of dictatorships in order to dissolve them. There are many weaknesses in dictatorships. But essentially, no political regime would continue without the support of the governed. On the other hand, if the people actively resisted and refused to cooperate with the government, the foundation would be undermined from below. On this point, Sharp's understanding is the same as Arendt's concept of power. Therefore, it seems certain that Arendt has provided him with a foundation for his theories on social change and nonviolent revolution.

5. Conclusion

Although I have written about Arendt's influence on theories of nonviolence, particularly on Sharp's theories of nonviolence, it is difficult to assess how great this influence is. There are many thoughts and ideas that have affected his theories. There are many sources of nonviolent theory, and to learn from the praxes of ordinary people is particularly important. He has learned from the tradition of political thought and successful historical examples. However, the new understanding of power conceived by Arendt is crucially important for the development of nonviolent theories.

It is certain that Arendt is not a believer in nonviolence, and she

(42) See Gene Sharp, *From Dictatorship to Democracy: A Conceptual Framework for Liberation*, London: Green Print Housmans, 2011, p. 88. According to Sharp, the booklet *From Dictatorship to Democracy* was written at the request of the late U Tin Maung Win, a prominent exile democrat who was then editor of *Khit Pyaing* (*The New Era Journal*). Although the request was to write an analysis focused only on Burma (Myanmar), Sharp had to write a generic analysis due to his lack of knowledge about Burma.

(43) *Ibid.*, p. ix.

seems rather skeptical of its effectiveness. In contrast, Sharp believes in the effectiveness of nonviolence. He stresses strategic nonviolence and has endeavored to spread the ideas of the strategic use of nonviolence. In spite of these differences, it is possible to find a linkage between them. This is the reason why I chose the concept of power as a key to link these two thinkers.

To achieve a better and more peaceful world, a new theory is needed in a new age. If we consider democratization radically, a new type of democracy must be nonviolent and based on the lives and attitudes of ordinary people. From the history of the development of nonviolent actions, we affirm that producing power among people in equal relationships is a key factor in creating and defending democracy.

This concept of power should be applied not only to political change from dictatorship to democracy but also to strengthen self-government in regions and organizations. It is of great importance to bear in mind that humans have the potential to create democratic power and change society from below.

VI

Hannah Arendt and Masao Maruyama:
The Meaning of Politics for Citizens

1. Introduction

A little more than forty years have passed since Hannah Arendt died in 1975, but it can be said that she had already established herself as one of the great thinkers in the history of political theory. This can be attributed to her ability to grasp the true meaning of politics through her experiences of surviving the political tumult of the 20th century and living through totalitarianism under Nazi Germany. She published many outstanding works in which she did not express her own experiences directly, but analyzed contemporary politics theoretically.

As one of the thinkers who revived the traditional mode of political theory, Arendt's works are well read among those specializing in Western political thought who consider her to be an original and brilliant thinker on par with Carl Schmidt. However, it is clear that at a time when the consciousness of affirming the expectations and revolutionary violence of socialism was still firmly held among Japanese intellectuals [(1)], Arendt

(1) Ichiyo Muto criticized Arendt's position at the time for lacking a critical perspective on the aspect of administrative violence in his book review on a Japanese translation of *Crises of the Republic* (Ichiyo Muto, "Yokuatsuteki Shisou to Muishiki no Gougan (Repressive Thought and the Unconscious Hubris)," *Asahi*

was sometimes viewed with suspicion because she regarded Nazism and Stalinism as belonging to the same category of totalitarianism. At that time the true value of her theory came to be recognized only by those who tackled political realities without prejudice.

Although the political theory of Hannah Arendt began to attract attention as an authentic subject matter from the 1990s, one of Japan's political scientists who had gained inspiration through reading Arendt's works since the 1950s was Masao Maruyama (1914–96). Maruyama was unquestionably the first figure to represent Japanese political science after the Second World War; a thinker who had a major impact on his readers during his lifetime and whose work, after his death, established his permanent status as a great scholar. He was a seminar student of Shigeru Nambara, a professor of Western political philosophy at the law faculty of Tokyo Imperial University.

Maruyama started his academic career as an assistant professor studying the history of Japanese political ideas as suggested by his mentor, the liberalist Nambara. Maruyama first became well known as a political scientist by carrying out comparative reflections on the history of Japanese political ideas using the concepts he learned in his studies of Western political thought.

Although his fundamental political views were formed under the influence of Max Weber and Carl Schmidt rather than that of Arendt, Maruyama entitled one of his books, *During the Wartime and the Postwar Period*, which draws from his articles and reviews spanning the period from his prize 1936 essay of his student years to articles written in 1957. It is clear that Arendt's book, *Between Past and Future*, was the inspiration behind its naming, as indicated in the book's postscript. (2) However, even if there

---

Journal, vol. 15, no. 34 (August 31, 1983), pp. 64–65).

(2) See Masao Maruyama, "Afterword," in *Senchu to Sengo no Aida: 1936–1957* (*During the Wartime and the Postwar Period: 1936–1957*), Tokyo: Misuzu Shobo, 1976, p. 635.

were some influential relationship between them, it was weak and one-sided from Arendt to Maruyama, since there is no trace of evidence that Arendt actually read Maruyama's writings.

It is significant that these two thinkers lived in roughly the same time and shared a common political experience — surviving World War II and working mainly after its end. As a Jew, Arendt experienced persecution, arrest, exile, and compulsory internment while she engaged in resistance against the Nazis. From his own army experience Maruyama also had a strong normative consciousness that Japanese fascism should not only be revealed but eradicated. Furthermore, he had experienced the atomic bombing of Hiroshima as a soldier based in Ujina, located in the southern district of Hiroshima City; this experience is not revealed in his work, but it was deeply rooted in his consciousness.

In order to return politics to ordinary citizens and to make it the everyday business of humans, it is important to consider what politics means for ordinary people and we must consider how to use traditional political theories in search of a better world. As Arendt suggests, we find ourselves between the past and the future. Therefore, it is important to engage in dialogue with the past by reading books written by great thinkers of the past. Within this framework, I focus on the theme of dialogue that Arendt and Maruyama made with the past and clarify how they formed their own theories by returning to the past, for much can be learned from the lessons of the past if we are to make the world a better place to live together in the future.

2. Hannah Arendt on the Meaning of Politics

Although we can neither change the past nor know the future, a human being who stands in between the past and the future, provided he or she understands the past in an accurate and meaningful way, is able to create a better future. In this sense, it is important to understand not only negative events in history but also capture and observe the essential features of these events.

In building a theoretical understanding, Arendt and Maruyama considered political matters from the historical tradition of Western political ideas. They also commonly focused on trying to understand the mechanism of governmental organization under which freedom is denied by the rule of ideology and by forcing people to do nothing but obey.

To reverse the politics of totalitarianism

As Arendt herself suggested, *The Origins of Totalitarianism* (1951) was an attempt to understand totalitarianism which, according to her, is an unprecedented form of government both in history and ideology. Analyses of Nazism or fascism have generally been made by the historical positivist method, which is common in the social sciences. As for political science, such a study is situated in the field of political history with specialists for each country in certain periods, and generally adopting the causal approach. Although the viewpoint of comparison is immanent in the study of politics, unlike the methods of history and political science, Arendt's analysis was phenomenological in going deep to grasp the essence of a political phenomenon itself.

When asked from where she came, Arendt once said, "If I can be said to 'have come from anywhere,' it is from the tradition of German philosophy." (3) She was proficient in five languages (English, German, French, Latin, and ancient Greek), had extensive knowledge of the history of Western ideas, and her thinking was clearly influenced by German philosophy, including that of Husserl and Heidegger, which enabled her to phenomenologically approach political matters.

Arendt's approach to totalitarianism took a macroscopic perspective in taking up and analyzing the most critical problems of her time. It was

(3) Hannah Arendt, "Eichmann in Jerusalem," (An Exchange of letters between Gershom Sholem and Hannah Arendt), *Encounter*, vol. 22 (January 1964), p. 53.

an attempt to tackle problems such as how to deal with events such as the mass murder of those who belonged to certain categories. To clarify the mechanism of totalitarianism was so important for Arendt that she could not bear to live without studying this theme. Her study of totalitarianism was clearly different from scientific inquiry, which chooses objects to which a method can be applied and consists of the accumulated results of such research.

Arendt was most active in the eight years from 1933 to 1940. As already stated in Chapter 2, during these years, as a Jew Arendt was deeply engaged in the resistance movement against the Nazis. Although in 1940 she was confined for over a month in a camp in Gurs, a small town in the Pyrenees Atlantic province, she fortunately escaped and reached New York via Lisbon in 1941 as a political refugee.

On the other hand, most people left behind in the Gurs camp were later transported to the Auschwitz concentration camp and murdered. Clarifying the dynamics of this history, which had led to the emergence of concentration camps, was, for Arendt, a work she could not put aside. Obviously, people with such an experience could not necessarily write a literary work, as Arendt did. Unlike many of those who wrote of their experiences directly as memoirs, Arendt had been thinking intensively and persistently about this particular phenomenon. This made it possible for her to describe the details of events based on facts, and with her, it could be done through philosophical knowledge and intensive study.

What Arendt did in *The Origins of Totalitarianism* (1951) was to find many elements from the historical facts of modern Europe that led to totalitarianism and then clarify the connections between them in order to elucidate the mechanism of totalitarian government. Although capitalism, racism, nation-state consciousness, bureaucracy, imperialism, and tribal nationalism are among the elements that led to totalitarianism in Germany, Arendt considered each of them separately. Even if she thought that some of these elements would not inevitably lead to the appearance of totalitarianism, she took up the task of understanding totalitarianism as "the burden of our time" and traced their roots back through European history to discover their relationships with totalitarianism.

Racism is the element that Arendt considered the most important and she believed that anti-Semitism was at the core of the Nazi ideology. Arendt certainly felt the threat of anti-Semitism as a Jew, but it was above all important to discover why such an ideology, in stark contradiction to the universality of human rights, was produced in Europe, considered the most advanced civilization at the time.

On the other hand, terror is employed by totalitarian states, where people are separated by the force of fear. The apparatuses of terror are the secret police and concentration camps. The fear of secret information changes relationships among people into those filled with suspicion. Nothing is more dangerous than having a friend in a terror-dominated state because protecting oneself is done by secretly informing on one's friends; moreover, if one does not confess the truth about a friend, by deciding to live according to one's conscience even if arrested and detained, one is placed in a dilemma: whether to refuse to confess, and thus risk death in one's own family, or to betray a friend and thus indirectly cause him or her to be killed. [4] There is no room for conscientious resistance. What terror destroys is rapport among human beings and the space for "acting in concert" (Edmund Burke). [5]

Arendt is a type of political theorist who not only understands the essence of political matters but also looks for original meaning in the fundamental concepts of politics within political realities. She found positive aspects of political concepts in the negative meaning of the phenomenon represented by totalitarian domination. From the viewpoint of political phenomena, totalitarianism is also one of various political forms, and totalitarian power is also a type of power, but the basic concepts of Arendt's

---

(4) See Hannah Arendt, *The Origins of Totalitarianism*, 3rd edition, New York: Harcourt, Brace & World, Inc., 1966, p. 452.

(5) *Ibid.*, p. 474.

political theory are constructed by reversing such negative phenomena to positive meanings. That is, politics is an activity among equals, a phenomenon of no-rule, while power is understood horizontally as it emerges among people who act in concert with others. This duality of political concepts arises in Arendt's thinking because of her intention to criticize political realities by supposing an ideal form of politics.

Arendt was not a pacifist but a realist who believed that military force was needed to fight the Nazis. Recognizing that totalitarianism as a form of government arose not only in Nazi Germany or Stalinist Soviet Union but also in other countries, she did not attribute the related phenomena to particular conditions in either country. Rather, she found political fundamentals by reversing those elements that totalitarian regimes denied, that is to say, public freedom, public space, and the plurality of human beings. (6)

Furthermore, she found cause for hope in that even totalitarianism could not deny such human conditions as love of freedom, natality, and plurality. Since she has a dualistic view and macroscopic viewpoints, her theory of totalitarianism became the starting point of her political theory of bringing politics back to ordinary people.

The citizen spirit for Arendt

Arendt does not use democracy as an ideal type of polity, since it is the rule of many people, and it has a tendency to lead to rule by public opinion. It also includes the notion of rule, while she wants to exclude the idea of rule from political matters and considers the condition of politics as a situation where anyone can live humanely together with others. Although the Greek *polis* is considered a model of politics, public space can appear at any time and at any place; therefore, the public space in Arendtian terms is not restricted to an area but can be formed beyond national borders. Moreover, although citizenship in the Greek *polis* was based on slave labor, Arendt's

(6) *Ibid.*, p. 466.

republicanism is a new type of civic republicanism based on participation in public space and equality among fellow citizens [(7)] which, of course, neither affirms any slave system nor excludes women from the public space. [(8)]

Generally speaking, students of political thought start from a deep study of great thinkers of the past. The study of politics must be undertaken by tackling the ideas of great thinkers and political realities. In the case of Arendt, except for her dissertation on Augustine, no thinker was taken up as the main subject of her monographs. Her thought is so original that she does not depend on any single thinker or school of thought but on her own thinking and experiences.

Unlike Leo Strauss, Arendt's political theory is not based on interpretations of great thinkers but rather chiefly aimed at investigating the meaning of the political phenomena of her time. It consists of the search for the fundamentals in which every human being can live his or her life humanely. However, her thought consists of constant dialogues in the tradition of Western political philosophy that began with Plato and Aristotle. Although she was influenced by Tocqueville and Kant, Socrates was the most important dialogue partner for Arendt.

Socrates was a special personage for Arendt, since he remained a permanent presence in her thinking and she was thus engaged in dialogue with him. As is well known, he did not write a single book, and hence his thoughts have been transmitted to us through his contemporaries, such as Plato, Xenophon, and Aristophanes. Since his thought is expressed most strongly in the works of Plato, her dialogue partner is the Socrates who appeared in these works. Arendt persistently tried to distinguish Socrates from Plato and sought a prototype of critical thinking in the deeds and

---

(7) See Iseult Honohan, *Civic Republicanism*, London: Routledge, 2002, p. 129.

(8) Although Arendt is similar with Aristotle in that she emphasizes the self-sufficiency of action, her republicanism is intended to reconstruct the public realm as a "*polis* without slaves." (See Dana R. Villa, *Arendt and Heidegger: The Fate of the Political*, Princeton: Princeton University Press, 1996, p. 25.)

speech of the former. Similar to Karl R. Popper, Arendt wanted to de-Platonize Socrates, since Socrates was a very important person for her in terms of the spirit of citizenship and the problem of conscience. On the contrary, Plato was shocked at the trial and execution of Socrates by Athenian citizens in 399 BC and positioned politics as a business of rule; thus, he is an object of critical consideration for her.

For Arendt, Socrates was a model citizen. He engaged in dialogue with his fellow citizens in the *agora* or other venues and was open to criticism by others. Socrates did not want to be a political leader, but sought out how to live in the public sphere. The public sphere is an intermediate space between the city and the household. The Athenian people could earn the right to be called citizens as long as they performed public duties in the political community, even if they did not directly engage in decision-making in the *polis*.

Like Socrates, Arendt was engaged in politics only for a short period, from 1933 to 1940. However, she was always concerned with politics. She talked about political events with friends and acquaintances. She replied to the unknown readers of her work and exchanged letters with them. After she fled to America, she never committed to politics as an actor, even though she observed events in her time and expressed opinions about them. She endeavored to do her best to perform the obligations of a citizen as a writer.

In Arendt's political theory, there are two aspects of the role of citizens: actors and spectators. These two aspects are interrelated. Politics at the macro level are conducted in the background of the world. In this respect, actors act under the silent pressure of the public.

If we pick up several normative points in the role of a citizen, the following points are important to bear in mind: (1) Spontaneity: Humans must be free to voluntarily engage in politics. One is engaged in politics based on his or her concerns. The freedom not to join politics must also be acknowledged. (2) Taking the initiative: This involves beginning something new and implementing the idea. Proponents have to pursue communal work to its conclusion and take responsibility for their deeds. (3) Open-mindedness: Citizens must foster open attitudes. Open-mindedness means being open to the criticisms of others. The attitude of cooperation with others, including unknown people, is also necessary. (4) Equality as equal relationships: It is important to place humans not in relationships of order and obedience. (5) Moral courage: One must behave out of his or her independent will. He who cares for the world has the right to participate in politics or, as Arendt stated, "only those as voluntary members of 'an elementary republic'" who "care for more than private happiness and are concerned about the state of the world, would have the right to be heard in the conduct of the business of the republic." [(9)]

Conscience works as a result of thinking, as a function of making one unable to do evil or commit injustice. [(10)] The reason citizens are accustomed to thinking this way is that one's speech and deed are always to be examined. For this purpose, one must have an inner space named "myself." According to Arendt, the faculty of willing rather than thinking leads humans to action. By virtue of the faculty of willing, one can start something new and open up a new future. Thinking is the faculty used to avoid evil. A human being deliberately desires to speak with fellow citizens.

Arendt gained conviction about the idea of politics by returning to the ancient Greek *polis*. Politics was a part of life for Greek citizens. According to Arendt, *polis* is the space of "free deeds and living words." [(11)] Socrates was open to hearing the opinions and criticisms of others. He lived his life according to his conscience, never contradicting himself. He never did evil or committed injustice and was democratic about exchanging opinions with others. In word and deed he lived consistently. A citizen spirit is that which lives consistently with one's words.

---

(9) Hannah Arendt, *On Revolution*, New York: Viking Press, 1963, p. 284.

(10) See Hannah Arendt, *The Life of the Mind*, vol. 1: *Thinking*, New York and London: Harcourt, Brace & Jovanovich, 1978, pp. 190–193.

(11) *On Revolution*, p. 285.

3. Masao Maruyama on the Concept of the Democratic Spirit

When considering the concept of citizens as independent subjects in political society, political theorists have to examine which kind of political organization is desirable. Although the form of political society was not explicitly investigated by either Maruyama or Arendt, political reality is criticized from the viewpoint of the state of desirable politics, and a kind of idea as *telos*(end) of political theory is shown in a hidden form. In the case of Arendt, it was republicanism, while for Maruyama, it was democracy; however, neither of these are ideal states of society but rather expressions of an idea.

The idea of democracy

In contrast with Arendt, Maruyama understood democracy as a valuable idea, positing it at the highest position among political principles. Prewar Japan was organized under the emperor system, and postwar Japan's political system was democracy based on the popular sovereignty principle. For Maruyama, August 15, 1945, was a turning point in Japan. Of course, the Japanese people did not embark on a revolution on August 15, but Maruyama called the day a moment of "bloodless revolution." (12) Although Japan accepted democratization as mandated by the Potsdam Declaration, it was an occupational policy that pushed forward Japan's democratization. Especially important was *how* to make the new Constitution of Japan, and Maruyama himself participated in a group at his working place, Tokyo Imperial University, tasked to research the problem. He went to great effort

(12) Maruyama describes August 15, 1945, as the day of "Japan's so-called bloodless revolution." (Masao Maruyama, "Wakaki Sedai ni Yosu: Ikani Manabi Ikani Ikubekika (To Younger Generations: How to Learn and How to Live?)" (1947) in *Maruyama Masao Shu* (*The Works of Masao Maruyama*), vol. 3, Tokyo: Iwanami Shoten, 1995, p. 83.)

to see that the new constitution would be established by Japanese people themselves.

However, democracy was not only a problem of political institutions but also one involving the ways of social life and the human spirit. According to Maruyama, democratization does not end at the level of institutions, but is a never-ending process of reforming human lifestyles or the structure of the human spirit. It is Maruyama's belief that democracy must be rooted in the foundations of liberalism. The ancient Greek democracy did not place the independent individual in any predominant position; only in modern times was respect for the individual established. In the case of Maruyama, the people-sovereignty theory of Western modern thought became the starting point of Japan's democratization. As shown by his endorsement of John Locke's political philosophy rather than that of Rousseau, he envisaged a type of democracy based on the democratic spirit of individuals.

By regarding democracy as a kind of lifestyle, Maruyama maintained that although Japan's social system was not a dictatorship it was authoritarian in nature, and he believed that the democratic principle must penetrate society as a whole. In his article entitled "A Letter to a Liberalist" (1950), Maruyama emphasized the necessity to establish democracy in the everyday life of citizens, stating that such ideologies as liberalism and democracy "are not produced out of the life experiences of the Japanese people." (13) For example, he questioned the reality of decisions even those reached by "discussion": "Over 100 meetings are held every day, which are far from mutual persuasion, and so can decisions made in such settings be considered a 'democratic' determination? In particular, when a hierarchical order between the top and the bottom is found among constituents, unless an upper-level person has the greatest self-restraint in power and impartial eyes, free discussion is instantly made a farce by various functions of *extra*-logical

(13) Masao Maruyama, "Aru Jiyushugisha eno Tegami (A Letter to a Liberalist)" (1950), in *Maruyama Masao Shu* (*The Works of Masao Maruyama*), vol. 4, Tokyo: Iwanami Shoten, 1995, p. 319.

coercion." [14]

This state of affairs shows how distant the reality of so-called democratic decisions is from the idea of democracy, although it is said that decisions are made by mutual persuasion. This condition implies that the function of political theory is to criticize realities from the standpoint of ideas, and for this purpose, one must have the ability to capture the essence of actual politics and criticize reality. This faculty is of such a nature that it requires not only scientists but also every citizen to learn on their own.

Maruyama was firmly convinced that democracy is unachievable if one does not become an independent individual; therefore, his democratic theory focuses on the state of human spirit. In order to root the democratic lifestyle in society, it is necessary that (1) each human being become an independent person and (2) one respect others as independent persons. [15] During the war, Maruyama formed his democratic thought from two liberal thinkers, Yukichi Fukuzawa and John Locke, as the sources of his dialogue partners.

Maruyama believed that democracy could not be achieved if the individual spirit was not sufficiently cultivated to become democratic. Although the freedoms of thought, faith, conscience, and the spirit of tolerance were formulated in modern European thought, their foundations are not found exclusively in Western civilization. According to Maruyama, it is crucially important in democracies to relativize a visible authority such as the law or the emperor with an invisible authority such as the truth or justice, and seek universality. Although even if universality can be sought, it can never be attained. Maruyama regarded democracy as a universal idea.

Therefore, we have to constantly fight against moves toward injustice and against undemocratizing forces in order to arrive at democracy. Such a struggle depends on the activity of an independent human being, who Maruyama considers to be a democratic citizen trying continuously to

---

(14) *Ibid.*, p. 323 (emphasis by Maruyama).

(15) See Masao Maruyama, *Jikonaitaiwa: 3 Satsu no Nōto kara* (*Self-reflective Dialogue: From 3 Notebooks*), Tokyo: Misuzu Shobo, 1998, pp. 10–11.

reshape him- or herself in order to come close to the idea of democracy.

The mentality sustaining the emperor system

Similar to Arendt, for Masao Maruyama, who lived under the ideology of the emperor system, the experience of fascism provided great momentum for his firm determination to explore the mechanism of Japanese fascism. Although he came to use the word "totalitarianism" later in the 1980s, Maruyama was interested in how such a monolithic ideology that centered on the emperor was formed.

Since he studied Western political ideas, he strived to describe political realties while always being conscious of comparison. As a student of the most elite high school at the time, The First High School in Tokyo, he attended a lecture by the journalist and liberalist Nyozekan Hasegawa and was arrested and detained for one night. While he was an associate professor at the law faculty of Tokyo Imperial University, he was drafted into the army, where he experienced violence and repression. These experiences motivated him to explore the mechanism of the emperor system.

Maruyama, who majored in political science and the history of Japanese political ideas, did not have any other way to conduct research other than using concepts and terms such as fascism and nationalism, concepts which were developed through the history of Western social sciences. However, in common with Arendt, he analyzed political realities both theoretically and historically.

Although he did not write a huge work on totalitarianism, as did Arendt, he released several noteworthy articles focusing on Japanese fascism. It was his treatise entitled "Theory and Psychology of Ultra-Nationalism" which attracted most people in the aftermath of World War II. It was written with the intention of escaping the spell of the emperor system after the war, and since it appeared in the monthly journal *Sekai* (*The World*), published by Iwanami Shoten, it was read widely among socially conscious people.

In this article, Maruyama clarified that the standard of values "that determined a person's position in society was based less on social function than on relative distance from the Emperor." (16) The emperor was at the top of the hierarchy of the Japanese political system and was the ultimate source of authority. According to Maruyama, "Nietzsche characterizes aristocratic morality as 'the pathos of distance' (*Pathos der Distanz*); for the ruling class of Japan, the consciousness of being separated from the 'humble' people increased in proportion with the sense of being near the ultimate value, that is, the Emperor." (17)

Maruyama's key concept of "transfer of oppression" means that by "exercising arbitrary power over those who are below, people manage in a downward direction the sense of oppression that comes from above, thus preserving the balance of the whole." (18) According to his understanding, this principle was expanded to include the international arena, as he stated, "This can be seen in the campaign in favor of invading Korea, which flared up directly after the Restoration, and in the subsequent dispatch of troops to Formosa." (19) Absolute value was expressed not in an individual person but within the sovereign, and thus ordinary people conducted themselves based not on their independent morality but on this type of social psychology.

Maruyama clarified the mechanism explaining why acts of atrocity were inflicted by ordinary people as follows: "The masses, who in ordinary civilian or military life have no object to which they can transfer oppression, should, when they find themselves in this position, be driven by an explosive impulse to free themselves at a stroke from the pressure that has been hanging over them. Their acts of brutality are a sad testimony to the Japanese system of

---

(16) Masao Maruyama, "Theory and Psychology of Ultra-Nationalism" (1946), translated by Ivan Morris, in *Thought and Behavior in Modern Japanese Politics*, Expanded Edition, ed. by Ivan Morris, Oxford: Oxford University Press, 1969 [1963], p. 13.

(17) *Ibid*., p. 13.

(18) *Ibid*., p. 18.

(19) *Ibid*., p. 18.

psychological compensation." [20] As Yukichi Fukuzawa radically criticizes this type of mentality as "attaching too great importance to power" [21] in his major work *An Outline Theory of Civilization* (1875), it is this type of spiritual structure that modern Japan inherited from the previous feudal society. Since modern Japan was formed as a centralized administrative state system whose center was the emperor, Maruyama thought free active consciousness was not formed because it was believed that the ethical mechanism which carries out goodness, truth, and beauty was embodied only in the emperor; rather that ordinary Japanese people were not considered capable of freely forming the conscience by which people normally regulate their actions.

However, the emperor, who was placed at the center of modern Japan, was also merely a traditional character, not a free actor, in contrast to the absolute monarchs in early modern European history. "Though the Emperor was regarded as the embodiment of ultimate value, he was infinitely removed from the possibility of creating values out of nothing. His Majesty was heir to an Imperial line unbroken for ages eternal, and he ruled by virtue of the final injunctions of his ancestors... It was only because his existence was inextricably involved in the ancestral tradition, in such a way that he and his Imperial Ancestors formed a single unit, that he was regarded as being the ultimate embodiment of internal values." [22] The center is understood not as "a single point but an axis of ordinates" that forms the massive "system of irresponsibilities" [23] whose center also lacked a sense of responsibility. Such

---

(20) *Ibid.*, p. 19.

(21) *Ibid.*, p. 18. See also Yukichi Fukuzawa, *An Outline of a Theory of Civilization* (1875), *The Thought of Fukuzawa*, vol. 1, revised translation by David A. Dilworth and G. Cameron Hurst III, Tokyo: Keio University Press, 2008, pp. 176–182.

(22) "Theory and Psychology of Ultra-Nationalism," p. 20.

(23) Maruyama uses this term in the context of criticizing the mentality of Japan's wartime leaders. (See Masao Maruyama, "Thought and Behaviour Patterns of Japan's Wartime Leaders" (1949), translated by Ivan Morris, in *Thought and Behavior in Modern Japanese Politics*, p. 128.)

a "system of irresponsibilities" can be applied not only to the emperor system in its political dimensions, but also to Japanese society in general.

On this point, how the materials of the Tokyo Trials clarified the mentality of military leaders is analyzed in an article entitled "Thought and Behaviour Patterns of Japan's Wartime Leaders" (1947). Maruyama explained that the subjects being judged were deficient in their decision-making processes. In making decisions, they were moved by an atmosphere of relative situations and by the urge to "escape to authority."

"Transfer of oppression" and "the system of irresponsibilities" were concepts created by Maruyama when he considered actual politics, and these were also realities to be conquered. The emperor system denies the free subject, which Maruyama considered as the most important problem. He is similar to Arendt in drawing out positive values from negative matters. However, unlike Arendt, Maruyama emphasizes human psychology. He thought much of the concept and function of authority because modern Japan has built such a mechanism that forces everybody into "voluntary obedience" to orders.

Consequently, a free subject could be formed only if we could remove that structure from Japanese society. This was the subject's problem, which Maruyama had to tackle in the first place after the end of World War II. Although Maruyama pushed himself into the study of the history of ideas in Japan, he called the period when he engaged in the research of contemporary politics a period of managing a "food stall," but I don't think it is necessary to take his words at face value. It seems to me that he earnestly practiced his work in political theory through an analysis of Japanese politics. By having begun to derive the pathology of modern Japan's political society immediately after the war, Maruyama began to form his prototype of a citizen as "a free subject" and "the subject who judges right and wrong, good and evil." Like Arendt, Maruyama himself engaged in thinking by "seeing the dark in the bright and conversely seeing the bright in the dark" [24] and his criticism of the mentality of the emperor system was carried out through the ideal of universal value.

Dialogue with Yukichi Fukuzawa

In the case of Maruyama, he seldom used the term "civil society" in the contemporary sense. Since he was influenced by the tradition of Marxist social science, Maruyama first understood civil society as a bourgeois society. Nonetheless, he had come to use the term "citizen" as a distinct concept from "bourgeois" after the war and became the most influential advocate of citizen-based democracy in Japan. Therefore, it is reasonable to search for various elements leading to the contemporary theory of civil society in the thoughts of Maruyama.

For Masao Maruyama, the most important dialogue partner was Yukichi Fukuzawa. This is related to Maruyama's primary intention, that is, how to create an independent spirit in Japan. Fukuzawa, whose thought Maruyama intensively studied during wartime and after the war, was a theorist of civil society as a "civilized society." The most important matter for Fukuzawa was civilization. To create a civilized society, it is necessary to foster an 'independent spirit of self-respect' in all people in Japan. This is why he decided on education as his vocation.

According to Maruyama, Fukuzawa was the original thinker in Japan. If originality means producing something from nothing, of course, Fukuzawa is not original; however, in the field of thought, originality does not mean generating a completely new thought but finding the most important elements in past thought and reshaping them into new ideas. In this sense, Fukuzawa was an unusual thinker in modern Japan. According to Maruyama, Fukuzawa was a "thinker about civil society" in that he emphasized

---

(24) *Jikonaitaiwa: 3 Satsu no Nōto kara* (*Self-reflective Dialogue: From 3 Notebooks*), p. 38.

interaction among people and dialogue with others. [25]

4. Coincidences between Two Thinkers

Arendt and Maruyama considered the importance of politics in small groups. They were commonly concerned with many actual problems and thought about the state of political society from a broad perspective. It is of great interest to find and consider the coincidences between these two thinkers.

Open-mindedness

The most important concept for both is the open-mindedness of the human spirit. By engaging in dialogue with Fukuzawa, Maruyama became aware of the importance of "the sense of others," which means thinking or feeling from another's viewpoint. A change in roles is necessary to achieve such a sense. According to Maruyama, the citizen should be "one party for one person" and should be an independent individual. Moreover, the citizen is a person who does not make politics an occupation for oneself like a lay Buddhist but always embraces a concern with politics.

Maruyama's image of citizens closely resembles Arendt's concept of citizens. This is because, for Arendt, the citizen is a singular being, an individual who cares for the world rather than for himself. The ordinary citizen is a human whose profession is not politics but who lives partly in the public sphere while being able to begin something new in cooperation with fellow citizens. The formation of citizenship must be considered important because it is closely related to the formation of civil society.

---

(25) See Masao Maruyama, "Fukuzawa Yukichi no Tetsugaku: Tokuni sono Jijihihan tono Kanren (The Philosophy of Yukichi Fukuzawa: Focused on his Criticism of Current Events)" (1947), in *Maruyama Masao Shu* (*The Works of Masao Maruyama*), vol. 3, p. 196.

Bringing back politics to ordinary citizens

Arendt's political theory did not measure politics with a scale of labor or work, but from the level of action. Although one must admit that such a viewpoint is too weak to influence politics at the national level, it becomes important at a time when an individual is to be esteemed. For that purpose, one must get politics back to one's own life, and realize an equal relationship in every dimension of society and make democracy a nonviolent way of life. This is the reason why Arendt recovered the hidden meaning of political concepts such as politics, power, violence, and freedom, as Margaret Canovan stated, "She manages to find within our existing language more shades of meaning than we are commonly aware of when we use different words as synonyms." (26)

Arendt redefined politics as action. This is the type of politics we can consider possible in civil society, where people cooperate with each other, and it can be said that citizen action can make politics everyday business. Therefore, present-day civil society can be regarded as a space for "politics as action," and a space of "free deeds and living words" is to be created everywhere. From this point of view, human beings are expected to open new possibilities through spontaneous and creative attempts that until now have been unpredictable.

Foundations of citizenship and civil society

Arendt's political theory influenced the rebirth of the concept of civil society in the 1980s. She did not use the term civil society, and she was against the conformity and uniformity in society that came from the ancient Greek household (*oikos*). However, the present concept of civil society is almost the same as the political community (*politikē koinōnia*) in ancient Greece, where Socrates lived with his fellow citizens.

It is important to recognize that society has two functions: (1) socializing

(26) Margaret Canovan, *The Political Thought of Hannah Arendt*, London: J. M. Dent & Sons, 1974, p. 10.

people and shaping human consciousness in a solid mold that is dominant in society and (2) providing people with places to meet unknown people and thus create new personal networks. In the second sense, society has the potential to connect individuals to public matters. Although Arendt valued public space for politics, public space can now emerge everywhere in society, even in the form of social activities. She suggested the importance of something which is in between (*inter-est*), "which lies between people and therefore relates and binds them together. Most action and speech [are] concerned with this in-between, which varies with each group of politics, so that most words and deeds are *about* some worldly objective reality in addition to being a disclosure of the acting and speaking agent." (27) Although interest is usually economically defined, it is a common concern in which people are interested. It may be a symbol of public affairs around which citizens gather and act in concert.

It is, therefore, possible to extend Arendt's concept of action to the sphere of civil society. From her point of view, civil society is an intermediate domain that belongs to neither the state nor the private domain. What she suggests in relation to the view of society as a semi-public sphere is that this sphere is important for fostering the individuality and diversity of human beings. Her book *Rahel Varnhagen* (1959) and her article "Reflections on Little Rock" (1959) are important works that portray society as an intermediate space, or a mixed domain of the private and the public, in contrast to her conception of society in *The Human Condition* (1958). In *Rahel Varnhagen*, the salon is a semi-public space, while in "Reflections on Little Rock" society is defended by her as a realm enabling the fostering of diversity. (28)

---

(27) Hannah Arendt, *The Human Condition*, Chicago: The University of Chicago Press, 1958, p. 182 (emphasis by Arendt).

(28) See Hannah Arendt, *Rahel Varnhagen: Lebensgeschichte einer deutschen Jüdin aus der Romantik*, München: Piper & Co. Verlag, 1959, pp. 26–47; "Reflections on Little Rock," *Dissent*, vol. 6, no. 1 (Winter 1959), p. 51.

According to Arendt, “acting in concert” can generate power among citizens, and its condition is defined by humans living together. The political exists ubiquitously and combines people to solve social problems. By cooperating and acting together in everyday life with others, people can become citizens and society works as places for people to meet each other. If the spirit of citizenship is open-mindedness, civil society must be an open society. The formation of an open mind is conditioned by civic culture, which is fostered by the tradition and history of a city or region where one has had memories worth discussing.

5. Conclusion

Political theory must be critical with regard to political realities to improve the human condition. As Maruyama recognized, realities cannot be criticized by other realities; rather it is ideas that can criticize political realities. The most important function of political theory is to set up ideas that are valid for all humankind. Equality and freedom are ideas introduced by great thinkers in modern times.

The concepts of the political, politics, and power are crucial in contemporary political theory. In contrast to Carl Schmidt, Arendt's concept of politics is not antagonistic but collaborative. Her thinking places emphasis on ordinary people and bringing politics back to them. She shares Maruyama's view of politics in the places where people live.

Traditional political theory focuses on the problem of creating a stable and safe order on earth. However, political theory, which is represented by such great thinkers as Plato, Hegel, and Marx, somehow had an impact on the emergence of totalitarianism or dictatorship.[29] They wished to establish a perfect society without inconsistency, aiming at a world of the individual

(29) See Karl R. Popper, *The Open Society and Its Enemies*, vol. 1: *The Spell of Plato*, vol. 2: *The High Tide of Prophecy: Hegel, Marx and the Aftermath*, Fifth edition (revised), London: Routledge & Kegan Paul, 1966 [1945].

in harmony with the whole; however, history has proved that while trying to make heaven on earth, believers of such ideologies as racism or communism have made hell on earth. For this reason, in the 20th century, political theory abandoned the project of creating a perfect society and instead sought a better world and a better society, as did Arendt and Maruyama. Contemporary political theorists have continued in dialogue with past great thinkers and have tried to recover hidden meanings in past occurrences. Political theory has to focus on how to make this world better and more peaceful than it is now.

Political theory now has to seek citizen-based politics; while modern political theory focuses on the theory of sovereignty, contemporary political theory focuses on the concept of power. In this vein, contrary to the ordinary understanding of power, namely, the vertical concept of power, Arendt understood power as a horizontal force, providing the potential for people to act in concert as equals. This could be referred to as "people power," which can influence political decisions at the national level and start a new movement to influence the present conditions of the world. One is not forced to participate in politics, but those who are more concerned about 'the state of the world' than about private affairs will voluntarily take part in public affairs. Public action must be voluntary and regarded as an integral part of everyday life for everyone.

Special attention must be given to the positive meaning of political concepts in ordinary language. It is also necessary to create new concepts to clarify new experiences. Examples of such concepts are "people power," which comes from Arendt's concept of power, and "the sense of others," to which Maruyama ascribed special meaning, that is, to think and feel from the position of others. Maruyama emphasized this concept because, although it seemed to him that the Japanese people lacked it, it is crucially important for the democratic way of life. If we are to bring politics back to people, we must take back and develop the authentic meanings of political concepts. This is one of the tasks of political theory and the reason why we must regard it as the most important field of academic study for building a better world.

References

[Books and Articles]

Arendt, Hannah, "What Is Existenz Philosophy?" *Partisan Review*, vol. 13, no. 1 (Winter 1946).

Arendt, Hannah, *The Human Condition*, Chicago: The University of Chicago Press, 1958.

Arendt, Hannah, "Epilogue: Reflections on the Hungarian Revolution," in *The Origins of Totalitarianism*, Second enlarged edition, New York: World Publishing Co., Meridian Books, 1958.

Arendt, Hannah, *Rahel Varnhagen: Lebensgeschichte einer deutschen Jüdin aus der Romantik*, München: Piper & Co. Verlag, 1959.

Arendt, Hannah, "Reflections on Little Rock", *Dissent*, vol. 6, no. 1 (Winter 1959).

Arendt, Hannah, *Between Past and Future*, New York: The Viking Press, 1961.

Arendt, Hannah, On Revolution, New York: The Viking Press, 1963.

Arendt, Hannah, *Eichmann in Jerusalem: A Report on the Banality of Evil*, New York: The Viking Press, 1963.

Arendt, Hannah, "Eichmann in Jerusalem," (An Exchange of letters between Gershom Sholem and Hannah Arendt), *Encounter*, vol. 22 (January 1964).

Arendt, Hannah, *The Origins of Totalitarianism*, 3rd edition, New York: Harcourt, Brace & World, Inc., 1966 [1951].

Arendt, Hannah, *Men in Dark Times*, New York: Harcourt Brace & Jovanovich, 1968.

Arendt, Hannah, *Crises of the Republic*, New York: Harcourt Brace Jovanovich, 1972.

Arendt, Hannah, "Sonning Prize acceptance speech" (1975), used as a Prologue to a posthumous collection of her work entitled *Responsibility and Judgement*, edited and with an introduction by Jerome Kohn, New York: Schoken Books, 2003.

Arendt, Hannah, *The Life of the Mind*, vol. 1: *Thinking*, New York and London: Harcourt, Brace & Jovanovich, 1978.

Arendt, Hannah, *Lectures on Kant's Political Philosophy*, ed. by Ronald Beiner, Sussex: The Harvester Press, 1982.

Arendt, Hannah/Jaspers, Karl, *Hannah Arendt/Karl Jaspers Briefwechsel 1926-1969*, hrsg. von Lotte Köhler und Hans Saner, München: Piper, 1985.

Arendt, Hannah, *Was ist Politik?: Fragmente aus dem Nachlass*, hrsg. von Ursula Ludz; Vorwort von Kurt Sontheimer, München: Piper, 1993.

Arendt, Hannah, *Essays in Understanding 1930-1954*, edited by Jerome Kohn, New York: Harcourt Brace & Company, 1994.

Arendt, Hannah/McCarthy, Mary, *Between Friends: The Correspondence of Hannah Arendt and Mary McCarthy, 1949-1975*, edited by Carol Brightman, New York: Harcourt Brace & Company, 1995.

Arendt, Hannah/Blücher Heinrich, *Hannah Arendt/Heinrich Blücher Briefe 1936-1968*, hrsg. von Lotte Köhler, 1996.

Arendt, Hannah, *Denktagebuch, 1950 bis 1973*, hrsg. von Ursula Ludz und Ingeborg, Nordmann, in Zusammenarbeit mit dem Hannah-Arendt-Institut, Dresden, Piper, 2002.

Bay, Christian, "Civil Disobedience," in the *International Encyclopedia of the Social Sciences*, Ⅱ, 1968.

Blum, Jack, "Heinrich Bluecher 1899-1970" (a memorial article), *St. Stephen's Alumni Magazine*, November 1970.

Canovan, Margaret, *The Political Thought of Hannah Arendt*, London: J. M. Dent & Sons, 1974.

Canovan, Margaret, *Hannah Arendt: A Reinterpretation of Her Political Thought*, Cambridge and New York: Cambridge University Press, 1992.

Cohen, Carl, "Essence and Ethics of Civil Disobedience," *Nation*, No. 198, March 16, 1964.

Cohen, Carl/Freeman, Harrop, A./Haag, Ernest Van den, "Civil Disobedience and the Law," *Rutgers Law Review*, vol. 21 (Fall, 1966).

Delanty, Gerard, *Citizenship in a Global Age*, Buckingham: Open University Press, 2000.

Ettinger, Elźbieta, Hannah Arendt・Martin Heidegger (New Haven and London: Yale University Press), 1995.

Fukuzawa, Yukichi, *An Outline of a Theory of Civilization* (1875), *The Thought of Fukuzawa*, vol. 1, revised translation by David A. Dilworth and G. Cameron Hurst III, Tokyo: Keio University Press, 2008.

Gandhi, Mohandas Karamchand, "Civil Disobedience," (*Young India*, August 4, 1921), in *The Collected Works of Mahatma Gandhi*, vol. 21, New Delhi: Publications Division, Ministry of Information and Broadcasting, Government of India, 3rd revised edition, 2000 [1967].

Gay, Peter, *Weimar Culture: The Outsider as Insider*, New York: Harper & Row, 1968.

Germino, Dante, *Beyond Ideology: The Revival of Political Theory*, Chicago: University of Chicago Press, 1967.

Gregg, Richard B., *The Power of Nonviolence*, Philadelphia: J. B. Lippincott, 1934.

Grunenberg, Antonia, "Einleitung," in *Totalitäre Herrschaft und republikanische Demokratie: fünfzig Jahre The Origins of Totalitarianism von Hannah Arendt*, hrsg. von Antonia Grunenberg unter Mitarbeit von Stefan Ahrens und Bettina Koch, Frankfurt am Main: P. Lang, 2003.

Hobbes, Thomas, *Leviathan*, edited with an introduction by J. C. A. Gaskin (The Worlds Classics), Oxford: Oxford University Press, 1996 [1651].

Honohan, Iseult, *Civic Republicanism*, London: Routledge, 2002.

Jay, Martin, "Hannah Arendt: Opposing Views," *Partisan Review*, vol. 65, no. 3 (1978).

Jefferson, Thomas, *The Complete Works of Thomas Jefferson: Autobiography, Correspondence, Reports, Messages, Speeches and Other Official and Private Writings*, ed. by Henry Augustine Washington, Madison & Adams Press (Kindle Edition), 1984.

Locke, John, *Two Treatises of Government*, a critical edition with an introduction by Peter Laslett, 2nd edition, reprinted with amendments, Cambridge University Press, 1970 [1690].

Maruyama, Masao, "Theory and Psychology of Ultra-Nationalism" (1946), translated by Ivan Morris, in *Thought and Behavior in Modern Japanese Politics* (Oxford in Asia college texts), Expanded edition/ed. by Ivan Morris, Oxford: Oxford University Press, 1979 [1963].

Maruyama, Masao, "Wakaki Sedai ni Yosu: Ikani Manabi Ikani Ikubekika (To Younger Generations: How to Learn and How to Live?)" (1947) in *Maruyama Masao Shu* (*The Works of Masao Maruyama*), vol. 3, Tokyo: Iwanami Shoten, 1995.

Maruyama, Masao, "Fukuzawa Yukichi no Tetsugaku: Tokuni sono Jijihihan tono Kanren (The Philosophy of Yukichi Fukuzawa: Focused on his Critisism of Current Events)" (1947), in *The Works of Masao Maruyama*, vol. 3, Iwanami-shoten, 1995.

Maruyama, Masao, "Thought and Behaviour Patterns of Japan's Wartime Leaders" (1949), translated by Ivan Morris, in *Thought and Behavior in Modern Japanese Politics*.

Maruyama, Masao, "Aru Jiyushugisha eno Tegami (A Letter to a Liberalist)" (1950), in *Maruyama Masao Shu* (*The Works of Masao Maruyama*), vol. 4, Tokyo: Iwanami Shoten, 1995.

Maruyama, Masao, "Afterword," in *Senchu to Sengo no Aida: 1936–1957* (*During*

the Wartime and the Postwar Period: 1936–1957), Tokyo: Misuzu Shobo, 1976.
Maruyama, Masao, *Jikonaitaiwa: 3 Satsu no Nōto kara* (*Self-reflective Dialogue: From 3 Notebooks*), Tokyo: Misuzu Shobo, 1998.
Muto, Ichiyo, "Repressive Thought and Unconscious of Haughtiness," *Asahi Journal*, vol. 15, no. 34 (August 31, 1983).
Oakeshott, Michael, *Experience and Its Modes*, London: The Cambridge University Press, 1933.
Popper, Karl R., *The Open Society and Its Enemies*, vol. 1: *The Spell of Plato*, vol. 2: *The High Tide of Prophecy: Hegel, Marx and the Aftermath*, Fifth edition (revised), London: Routledge & Kegan Paul, 1966 [1945].
Powers, Roger S., "Sharp, Gene," in *Protest, Power, and Change: An Encyclopedia of Nonviolent Action from ACT-UP to Women's Suffrage*, editors, Roger S. Powers, William B. Vogele; associate editors, Christopher Kruegler, Ronald M. McCarthy, New York and London: Garland, 1997.
Randle, Michael, *Civil Resistance*, London: Fontana Press, 1994.
Rawls, John, *A Theory of Justice*, Cambridge, Massachusetts: Belknap Press of Harvard University Press, 1971.
Sano, Shoji, *Vorantia wo Hajimeru Maeni: Shiminkoekikatsudo* (*Before Beginning Volunteer Activity: Citizen Public-interest Activity*), Tokyo: Koujinnotomo-sha, 1994.
Sharp, Gene, *Exploring Nonviolent Alternatives*, Boston: Porter Sargent Publishers, 1970.
Sharp, Gene, *The Politics of Nonviolent Action*, Part 1, Boston: Porter Sargent Publishers, 1973.
Sharp, Gene, *Gandhi as a Political Strategist: with Essays on Ethics and Politics*, Boston: Porter Sargent Publishers, 1979.
Sharp, Gene, *Making Abolition of War a Realistic Goal*, New York: World Policy Institute, 1980.
Sharp, Gene, *There Are Realistic Alternatives*, Boston: The Albert Einstein Institution, 2003.
Sharp, Gene, *From Dictatorship to Democracy: A Conceptual Framework for Liberation*, London: Green Print Housmans, 2011.
Thoreau, Henry D., "Resistance to Civil Government," in *Reform Papers*, ed. by Wendell Glick (*The Writings of Henry D. Thoreau*), Princeton: Princeton University Press, 1973.
Villa, Dana R., *Arendt and Heidegger: The Fate of the Political*, Princeton: Princeton University Press, 1996.

Young-Bruehl, Elisabeth, Hannah Arendt: For Love of the World, New Haven and London: Yale University Press, 1982.

[Manuscripts]

Arendt, Hannah, "Political Experiences in the Twentieth Century," lectures, Cornell University, 1965, in *The Papers of Hannah Arendt*, at the Library of Congress, Washington, D.C.

Blücher, Heinrich, "Perpetual Motion. Some Tests of the Political Structures of Nazism," in *The Papers of Hannah Arendt.*

Blücher, Heinrich, "Nationalsozialismus und Neonationalismus," in *The Papers of Hannah Arendt.*

Blücher, Heinrich, "The Common Core Course," Introduction to the Common Course, delivered on November 16, 1952, and stored at Bard College Library, Annandale-on-Hudson.

Blücher, Heinrich, "Socrates," Lecture I: (In Two Parts), April 30, 1954, Two Lectures delivered at New School for Social Research, and stored at Bard College Library.

Blücher, Heinrich "Jesus of Nazareth," Lecture I, delivered at New School for Social Research, May 21, 1954, and stored at Bard College Library.

Notes:

1 Arendt's unpublished works are contained in *The Papers of Hannah Arendt* archived at the Library of Congress, Washington, D.C., and Blücher's lecture manuscripts and papers are archived at the main library of Bard College and in the *Family Papers of The Papers of Hannah Arendt.*

2 *The Papers of Hannah Arendt* can be accessed through the homepage of the Library of Congress (http://memory.loc.gov/ammem/arendthtml/arendthome.html), and Blücher's lectures are also open to read and be listened to through the *Blücher Archive*, Bard College (http://www.bard.edu/bluecher/listen.php).

The Political Theory of Hannah Arendt
In Search of Humane Politics

Published on June 25, 2021

Author	Toshio Terajima
Publisher	Fukosha Publishers Ltd.
	1-3-2 Kanda-sarugakucho, Chiyoda-ku, Tokyo
	101-0064 JAPAN
	Phone & Fax: 81-3-6672-4001
Printing office	Chuo Seihan Printing Corporation

 ISBN978-4-86258-140-2